LIAISON PILOT

LIAISON PILOT

by
James R. Bryce

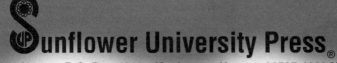
Sunflower University Press®
1531 Yuma • P.O. Box 1009 • Manhattan, Kansas 66505-1009 USA

ISBN 0-89745-266-6

Sunflower University Press is a wholly-owned subsidiary
of the non-profit 501(c)3 Journal of the West, Inc.

Contents

Technical Sergeant James R. Bryce in front of a Stinson L-5 Sentinel, Grenoble, France, 1944.

Preface

WHEN ASKED WHAT I did in World War II, I have always answered, with pride, "I was a liaison pilot." Almost every time, the question would then be asked, "What was a liaison pilot?"

I served in the U.S. Army Air Forces — we still often called it the "Air Corps" — from August 1, 1942, to September 9, 1945, and kept a diary, periodically recording many interesting events in detail. When I was shipped overseas, I soon realized that my participation would be a life-altering experience. I began writing letters on an almost daily basis to my mother and grandmother, describing my activities.

I assumed that the U.S. Army censor would delete anything that might be a breach of security, or a benefit to the enemy, if my letter were to fall into their hands. My grandmother, however, had received only two letters that showed the slice of a censor's scissors. She had kept all my letters — every one of them — in scrapbooks. When she died, they came into my possession. I found she even had carefully pasted the envelopes to the pages, with my letters inside.

My military pilot logs have been absolutely invaluable and instrumental in establishing an exact time line of my service years. Coupled with my diaries and the letters to my grandmother, they jogged my memory regarding long-forgotten events. As a result, this narrative is based almost entirely on documented facts and a vivid recollection of some of my wartime experiences.

I hope the reader will find the answer to the question, "*What* was a liaison pilot?"

Chapter 1

I DID NOT LIKE the Vultee BT-13 Valiant basic trainer the first time I walked up to it and had a good look. The aircraft looked too heavy to fly, the propeller looked too small, and the large glass canopy over the tandem cockpits looked like some nursery man's private petunia garden in a hothouse.

I had just arrived at Perrin Field near Sherman, Texas, in early November 1942 for Basic Training after completing my Primary Flight Training at the Wilson-Bonfils Flying School in Chickasha, Oklahoma. This was my first encounter with the aircraft in which I would fly during Basic. My flight instructor motioned for me to climb up onto the wing, slide the canopy back, and get into the front cockpit.

My parachute, hanging under my rear end, pulled me backward off balance, and I had a hard time sliding the canopy open. When I peered inside, I did not like what I saw — there was too much room. Everything was too big. The stick looked like the wrong end of a baseball bat, and the rudder pedals appeared to have been

James R. Bryce learned the rudiments of flying in the Fairchild PT-19 Cornell, during his Primary Flight Training at Wilson-Bonfils Flying School in Chickasha, Oklahoma, October 1942.

designed for King Kong. I crawled over into the seat and settled my parachute into place. I felt like I was in a glass-covered barn.

"I'll take her up first," the instructor's voice came over my intercom. "After you get a feel for the aircraft, I'll let you take over for a few maneuvers. I want to see what you learned in Primary Flight School."

I already had a feel for this aircraft. I didn't like it!

I had misgivings about becoming a fighter pilot — "off we go into the wild blue yonder. . . ." The battle cry was beginning to sound a little like baloney. I had laid awake several nights thinking that there was an experienced German pilot somewhere out there who was going to try to kill me in a few months.

I had admired the little Fairchild PT-19 Cornell primary trainer, in which I had learned the first rudiments of flying. It was a low-wing monoplane with smooth, elegant lines. The tandem cockpits were small and fit nicely around my body. I could see everywhere out of the open cockpit.

But in the BT-13, I sat so far down in the cockpit that when I closed the canopy, I couldn't see anything ahead. My visibility was limited to straight up and sideways. Then there was the noise. When the engine revved up, the inside of the cockpit sounded like a foundry. According to my pilot log, I spent a total of 8 hours and 40 minutes flying time in that big bucket of rivets.

During my Basic Training, I had two close calls, now known as "character builders." I was nearly killed twice. The first time was caused by my instructor. He was a pilot who liked to keep the aircraft trimmed so that the stick would remain in a neutral position, even when the aircraft was gliding in for a landing. Once, while we were coming in, I was at the controls and had no idea what was going on in the rear cockpit. Had I been more experienced, I guess I could have felt the stick soften as we glided down, but I was concentrating on my descent. I hit the runway too hard and bounced. Then I did exactly what I was supposed to do. I pushed the throttle full forward to abort the landing and go around again. The aircraft took off with a roar and headed almost straight up, approaching stall speed.

"*Get the nose down!*" my instructor yelled over the intercom. I tried to push the stick forward, but it was as tight as if it were bolted to the floor.

A Vultee BT-13 basic trainer similar to the one James R. Bryce flew at Perrin Field near Sherman, Texas, in early November 1942.
Confederate Air Force brochure, 1970

"Get it down! Get it down!" he screamed, and I felt the aircraft begin to stall.

Then, with both of us pushing as hard as we could on the stick, I felt the aircraft dip forward and begin to mush downward. Within ten feet of the runway the plane began to catch some air and move up again. That had been my closest brush with death.

The instructor took over the BT-13, circled the field, and landed. We climbed out of the aircraft and walked separately to the ready room. Not a word was spoken of the incident, then or ever after.

On November 24, 1942, I had my second close call during my solo flight in the BT-13. By that time, I had completed about seven hours of training in the aircraft. I knew that any day my instructor would crawl out and tell me to take the plane around.

He chose an auspicious moment. The night before, a student shooting night landings had been killed in a crash at the end of the runway during his approach to the auxiliary field. The next morning my instructor told me to fly to the crash site. We landed right over the smoking remains of the aircraft. I pulled up to the flight line and the instructor climbed out.

"Take her around," he said. That was the first time he had spoken to me that morning. I knew from the tone of his voice that this was a make-or-break flight.

I taxied the BT-13 to the end of the runway, lined up, and pushed the throttle to the stop. I had no problem with the takeoff. But as I climbed to 500 feet, I knew I was not ready to take the aircraft out on my own. I still did not like the plane; I could not get a feel for it and, above all, I was scared of it.

When I had soloed the Fairchild PT-19, I had let out a yell of pure joy when I reached my altitude in the traffic pattern. I felt I could take it up on my own and really learn to fly. I had been happy. In the Vultee BT-13, I felt that if I succeeded in this solo flight I would face a future of danger and ineptness. I was not happy.

I circled the field and went into my approach. Passing over the remains of the aircraft, I glanced out the side of the Vultee and watched the smoking wreckage pass beneath me. I knew what had happened. The student had approached too slowly and had stalled out before he was in a landing position.

I sure was not going to stall out. I eased the throttle forward, gaining some speed. As the aircraft eased downward I pulled the stick back and floated along the landing strip. I glanced out the side of the canopy and saw a clump of trees bordering the boundary of the field. I knew I was approaching the end of the strip, and one thought crossed my mind. "You're on the ground. *Stay there!*"

I pulled the stick all the way back and cut the throttle. The BT-13 fell to the runway and bounced. I held on to everything I had and hit the brakes. The tail rose into the air, then dropped back down. I looked out the side of the canopy and could see that I had stopped at the end of the runway. I taxied back to where my instructor waited.

"We're going to put some more work on your landings," was all he said.

During Basic Training I had heard rumors about liaison training; however, we cadets all had big dreams to fly fighters and bombers. And, at any rate, no one seemed to know exactly what a liaison pilot's job might be; one possibility was working as a spotter for the artillery, flying those little Piper Cubs. But an aviation cadet would be aghast if he had to fly such a lowly little aircraft.

I flew the Vultee BT-13 about three more hours. My landings did not improve, and I did not know then if I had been washed out of that phase of training; but I also did not want to find out. I concluded that the best way to survive was to grab the initiative while it was still available. I still wanted to fly, and that little Piper Cub seemed to be the answer to my problems.

Instead of going to the flight line one morning, I went to headquarters. I applied for transfer to liaison pilot training — one of the smartest moves I ever made.

Chapter 2

WE HAD BEEN coddled as aviation cadets, as we were supposed to be gentlemen in the making. We had a propeller insignia attached to the peaks of our caps. We had been provided with certain amenities, such as more space in the barracks and better service in the cafeteria. We had taken calisthenics separated from the so-call "riffraff" — the enlisted men — whom we had looked down upon.

The minute I transferred, I was moved from the cadet barracks to the enlisted men's barracks on the other side of the base, well away from the activities of the flying cadets. I became a Buck Private. This was not a demotion, because I had no rank as a cadet. But I became a member of the riffraff, and I loved it. Trying to fly that Vultee-BT 13 had been a real burden for me.

I was sent to a Replacement Depot, which we called a "repple-depple." Literally thousands of soldiers were waiting to be transferred to new assignments. While we waited, we were farmed out each morning to perform "make-work" tasks. We had roll call outside the barracks before dawn and 30 minutes of calisthenics. Then some of us were assigned to certain jobs; the rest were marched off to do close-order drill all day.

One of my assignments was to examine the "French ditches" bordering the runway. I wondered what in the world a French ditch was. My detail marched out, and on the way to the runway we were given shovels. We arrived at the job site beside a concrete runway. We were told that under a six-inch cover of dirt there was a ditch filled with small rocks — a French ditch — a drainage system that directed water away from the runway.

The Sergeant in charge of my detail told us to remove the dirt so that the rocks could be inspected; he would return soon, and we had better show some progress.

He showed up about 10 a.m. We had removed a considerable amount of dirt, and a long line of rocks ran parallel to the runway. The Sergeant walked along, looking intently into the ditch we had dug. When he returned, we formed up and he called us to attention.

"You've done a good job, men," he said, as if it had been a highly, official assignment. "All the rocks are there. Now cover them up."

In early March 1943, I was shipped out to begin my liaison flight training. Five of us arrived at the airport, a mile or so north of Plainview, Texas, late in the afternoon, just before a blue blizzard — a cold, windy winter storm — came rolling down from the northwest. The airport was a flat, treeless pasture with no particular name. The landing strips were earthen paths marked by wooden stakes stuck in the ground; the barracks were thrown together like large crates.

The first night the incessant cold wind and dust blew through the barracks almost unrestrained. The place was heated only by one wood-burning stove placed at a center point in the barracks. I put my cot near the stove and started a fire.

When the chill had been broken, we five went to bed. Sometime during the night the fire went out, and I woke up freezing. I was too cold to get up and start it again, so I pulled everything I could find over me and dozed off. The next morning I awoke so hot I was almost roasted. Someone had filled the stove with wood and revived the fire.

At about 10 a.m., glider and liaison pilot trainees arrived and filled our barracks. The glider pilot trainees were there to learn the rudiments of flying before going on to glider training.

On March 30, 1943, I took my first flight with my instructor in a Piper Cub J-3, designated as an L-4 Grasshopper by the U.S. Army Air Forces. Everything seemed to fall into place. The L-4's 65-hp Continental engine produced the slow airspeed necessary for liaison training — it flew slow and landed slow. It was basically comfortable, though the rear cockpit was so close to the forward cockpit that the instructor's knees touched my rear end. But I knew I had made the right decision to transfer. Within an hour of flying time, the instructor crawled out and told me to solo.

Flying training just got easier. Every morning after breakfast we stood roll call, went to a class on navigation or some other appropriate subject, then walked to the flight line, crawled into an aircraft, and took off. We were supposed to log hours. Occasionally our instructor would go with us and we would do some aerobatics — that is, we would *try* to do some aerobatics. The Piper Cub was not designed for that task, but it was fun to try to get the plane to loop or roll.

I tried to loop the Cub several times and each time, as I gathered speed and pulled it up, the plane reached almost to the top of the loop and fell out into a mini-spin that was easy to control.

On one occasion we practiced night landings. Along one side of the dirt runway a string of lights provided us with a reference. We had no control tower, nor did we have radios. We were told to keep our head out, and watch for the running lights on the other aircraft. We simply took off about 30 seconds apart.

Quite a few planes were in the air at one time, and we could see the running lights of other aircraft as we circled the field. Actually, what we learned that night was to look in all directions and keep alert.

Our instructors were civilians. However, we were constantly reminded that we were in the U.S. Army. We had regular drills, we faced roll call, our calisthenics were led by an officer, and, of course, we had to salute our officers. But we were not cadets any more, and some of that earlier military ceremony in retrospect seemed a little ridiculous. We had learned our lesson the hard way.

After several weeks in training we were allowed a Saturday and Sunday off to go into town. This was a real break, and we needed it. But late one Saturday afternoon, several of our students, who had been drinking, met an officer on a street in Plainview. Instead of just saluting and going on their way, they made a big deal of the meeting. As I was told the story, they saluted repeatedly, saluted with their left hand, made silly remarks, and generally violated all the rules of decorum held dear to the military man.

Apparently the officer did nothing but return their salute and continue on his way.

The following Monday morning, half the squadron had bad hangovers. When we assembled for calisthenics, a small ritual took place. As we marched onto the field to perform our morning exercises, the officer who had been subjected to the indignity walked up with a chair and sat directly in front of our formation. He waved his hand toward the athletic director, who instructed us to do the exercise that requires you to jump up and spread your feet, while you raise your arms above your head, then lower your arms and bring your feet back together.

The director began to count cadence as we performed the exercise. He gradually increased the cadence, until we were going at an almost in-human speed. The officer in the chair sat quietly watching.

I thought the performance would never end. I had always been in good physical shape, and I did not have a hangover. But I began to fade. Yet, I managed to hold on and keep going, though I wondered when the torture would end.

Finally one of the students fainted from exhaustion. The officer in the chair rose, picked up his chair, and left without saying a word.

Although we were trained by civilians, they could not wash us out. That was the duty of a Lieutenant assigned to our base to check our progress as we advanced through our training, and to give the final check ride. When-ever a civilian instructor had a student who was not progressing as he should, he would direct the student to the Lieutenant for a check ride.

If a student found himself scheduled for a ride with the Lieutenant, that student knew he was in trouble. The wash-out rate was horrendous. For some reason I felt that the standards there for liaison pilots were higher than what I had experienced in Primary or Basic Training.

At the end of our training period at Plainview we were given a flight test by the Lieutenant. If we passed, we were automatically promoted to the rank of Staff Sergeant and allowed to pin a set of wings to our uniforms. I did not worry in anticipation of my final test flight with the Lieutenant. I felt comfortable in the Piper Cub and I had confidence in my ability to fly it. I was ready to go.

On April 5, 1943, I passed my U.S. Army Air Forces test flight. I was in the air for two hours and fifteen minutes. The Lieutenant tested me so completely that I was amazed with my own performance. When it was over, he shook my hand, said it was a good job, and wished me well. He was a pretty good officer.

We had no ceremony upon completion of the liaison flight training. No pretty girls pinned our wings on our chests. Mothers and fathers did not stand by with tears of pride in their eyes. Rather, upon graduation, each of us received two pages of our Personnel Orders: No. 6, E X T R A C T 14, the liaison pilot rating, and E X T R A C T 15, the rank of Staff Sergeant.

I bought a pair of liaison pilot's wings at the PX (Post Exchange), sat on my cot, and pinned them on my uniform. It was a very proud moment. From then until I was discharged, I never wore my uniform without them. I still have those wings.

Immediately after receiving our wings we were shipped out to New Cumberland Air Depot just outside Harrisburg, Pennsylvania. We were billeted in a hangar with several North American B-25 Mitchell bombers — named for the renowned General Billy Mitchell, the avid bombing proponent. Our cots were arranged along one wall near the aircraft. It would be several days before we would be assigned to our own planes, so we were ordered to study technical manuals, an utterly boring pastime.

There was a lot of coming and going of clerical personnel, and we had to fall in and answer several roll calls at odd times. We had no idea what was happening.

What we found out in a few days was that the U.S. Army Air Forces was in the process of activating the 72nd Liaison Squadron, which was to be my home for the duration of the war. And at this time I began to learn how to be a soldier.

While studying the tech manuals, we were also marching and performing calisthenics. One day we were called into formation. One of the officers asked if any of us could use a typewriter. That was my ticket out of drill. My hand shot up, and I was told to go to the orderly room. My first duty was to type up weekend passes for the entire squadron. However, I had to stay in the orderly room all weekend, in case I "was needed."

The cardinal rule in the Army was to never volunteer for anything. That was just one of many things I learned the hard way.

Chapter 3

ONCE I HAD MY wings and was a part of a
newly organized squadron, everything changed for
the better. We still observed stern discipline, met
roll calls, and did calisthenics, but we also finally flew a lot. We
each were assigned our own Piper Cub — a great boost for the
ego.

After breakfast and calisthenics we went to the ready room and
filed a flight plan for "local reconnaissance." We were supposed to
build up hours of flying time. Because we were pretty much on
our own, we performed many maneuvers and trips just for
pleasure.

One day an Infantry soldier, who had never been up in an aircraft, asked me to give him a ride. He had a jaw full of tobacco,
which he managed to keep pretty well under control. Lots of
billowy clouds were around on that beautiful morning, and I
climbed up and flew among them for a while. I found one with a
flat top and flew along above it until I reached the edge. Then I

rolled the Cub over and dove straight down. Through the clean morning air, we could see the earth 2,000 feet below. I gradually pulled out of the dive into straight-and-level flight.

I looked back at my passenger, who was grasping the struts. He was deathly white after having swallowed his chaw of tobacco. When we returned to the airfield, I had to help him out of the Cub. But I got a lucky break; he threw up on the ground and not in my aircraft.

On another occasion, a good friend led me on a flight over his home in Gettysburg. We flew about 300 feet above the ground, following a railroad. The countryside was beautiful, and we enjoyed the early morning flight.

Can a Piper Cub fly backward? I had heard that pilots had, indeed, flown the little aircraft "in reverse," but I hardly believed it. I had never seen it happen.

One beautiful morning I noticed a group of pilots in front of the ready room looking skyward. Sure enough there was a Piper Cub moving backward — very slowly. It can happen and it did. The explanation is simple. A Piper Cub can stay aloft at 40 miles per hour airspeed if handled very carefully to keep it from stalling. At 2,000 feet, this particular morning, there was a steady wind at about 45 miles per hour. The pilot had turned the aircraft into the wind, throttled back so that the aircraft was barely above stall speed, and slowly drifted backward across the airfield.

During my stay at New Cumberland, the activation of the 72nd Liaison Squadron was completed, and I flew the Piper Cub over 300 hours. One incident gave me the biggest laugh I had during my entire enlistment.

Every Saturday morning we had to stand inspection at 9 a.m., before we went on pass into Harrisburg. The idea was to see that everyone was spick-and-span and in the appropriate uniform before we left the post. Our inspection was a military ritual, performed the same way every time. We assembled on the east side of the hangar and remained at attention while our Commanding Officer and his staff looked us over very closely. When he was satisfied, we marched from beside the hangar toward the front of the building where, on a reviewing stand, some dignitaries stood.

When we reached the proper place, our First Sergeant yelled, "Columns right!" — whereupon we wheeled right in columns of four. We then marched across in front of the reviewing stand. When we reached the other side of the hangar, the First Sergeant again yelled, "Columns right!" We marched off out of sight and were dismissed to go into town.

But on this particular day our inspection performance did not quite work out that way. We all knew what we were supposed to do; we had done it many times before. But that morning, when we marched across in front of the reviewing stand, instead of yelling "Columns right!" as he always did, the First Sergeant yelled, "Columns *left!*" We all knew we were supposed to wheel *right*. We could not believe that we had been ordered *left*!

The entire formation dissolved into a mass of giggling, laughing nuts, trying to figure out what to do, stumbling all over each other. The entire mess, writhing and chortling, moved like an amoeba toward the side of the hangar. We knew one thing for sure, we had better get out of sight! The dignitaries on the reviewing stand were staring at us as if we were committing some horrid, forbidden act.

Once out of their line of vision, the First Sergeant got us back in formation. He had the look of a man about to face a firing squad. Our CO came off the reviewing stand and marched up to our formation. I cannot described the expression on his face. He did not know whether to laugh himself to death or to cry like a baby. He simply dismissed us, and we took off for town like scared rabbits.

I never heard if anything ever had been said about the matter. I guess our performance had been just too horrible to dwell upon.

In mid-June 1943, rumors began to circulate that we were going to move from New Cumberland to Reading, Pennsylvania. We were going to be checked out in the Stinson L-5 Sentinel, an aircraft we all looked forward to flying. The L-5 was larger than the Piper Cub, and was powered by an 185-hp Lycoming engine. It was a beautiful aircraft to look at. With a cruising speed of 115 mph, its wing flaps and slots enabled the aircraft to land at about 40 mph in a short distance.

Just after arriving in Reading, before I ever climbed into an L-5, I was assigned, with three other pilots, to ferry four Piper Cubs from Reading to Richmond, Virginia. On the way, we stopped to refuel at Washington National Airport, now Ronald Reagan Washington National Airport. What makes this notable is that Washington National was then — and still is — one of the busiest airports in the world. All manner of civilian and military aircraft flew in and out at all hours of the day and night.

We had no radio or any other signaling device in the Cubs, so when we approached the airport, we kept our heads up and proceeded toward the runway. I made my approach at a little over 40 miles an hour, which was a snail's pace for that airport. I heard a man yelling from the end of the strip. *"Go! Go! Go!"* he shouted, waving me on down.

I pushed the throttle forward and flew to the other end of the runway, where I landed and pulled off onto an exit ramp. The fact that I *flew* from one end to the other really puts the Piper Cub's landing capabilities in the proper perspective.

When I pulled up for fuel, I was placed in the proper perspective again. After the attendant had filled my tank I asked him for a TO (Technical Order) to sign. He laughed a little bit and said, "Forget it, Sergeant. I spill more gas than that on the wing when I fill up a B-24."

I was checked out in the Stinson L-5 in early July 1943. The tandem cockpits were roomy, the instruments were convenient, and the aircraft responded handily to the controls. The L-5 had more speed than the Piper Cub; it had been designed for straight-and-level flight at a relatively low speed.

I flew the dependable L-5 for the duration of the war. It was a very satisfying aircraft, and the more I flew it the better I liked it.

Our training at Reading Army Air Field was about the same as at New Cumberland. Each of us was assigned an L-5, and we were supposed to fly and accumulate hours. Occasionally, an officer would give us a test flight to see how we were doing. We usually could fly the aircraft better than the officer. No one ever worried about the check ride.

However, there were two changes from the previous training at New Cumberland: we were told to practice "dogfighting," and we were to work in the Link trainer, an early flight simulator.

Because our aircraft was not armed or designed for aerobatics, we questioned the motive behind the assigned dogfighting maneuvers. Was aggressive attack to be one of our duties? Well, we were ordered to dogfight, so we all took a crack at it.

For the first session, I teamed up with another pilot and we took off together. We climbed to about 4,000 feet. I waggled my wings, which was our signal to "attack." We had closed to about a mile of each other, and he attacked first — that is, he turned in my direction and flew toward me. I didn't know what he was supposed to do, and he didn't either. As he closed on me, I simply turned in another direction and he could not overtake me. I think he was trying to get on my tail. That's what we had been told to do.

I made a tight turn and tried to get behind him. I glanced at my altimeter. We were losing altitude. In no time, we were approaching 1,000 feet. Both of us knew that was too low to perform the maneuvers. Separating some distance, we began the slow climb to regain some altitude. We made one more attempt at dogfighting. I attacked him, but didn't come close. Again we lost altitude at a rapid rate.

The L-5 was a fine aircraft, but it had not been built for combat.

In the other addition to our training, we were exposed to the Link trainer, which was a mockup of an actual cockpit that simulated flying blind with the use of instruments. The Link training was not required, but, being a conscientious student, I decided to take advantage of the opportunity. I signed up for a couple of sessions, but I had trouble trying to keep the trainer from stalling out.

The L-5 aircraft had a turn-and-bank indicator and an airspeed indicator. I could have flown on these instruments for a short period of time, if I had taken further advantage of the Link training. A few times during my later liaison missions, I was in real trouble and could have used more knowledge of instrument flying.

In late July 1943, I had a ruptured appendix, which took me out of flying for almost three months. I was kept in bed for two weeks after the
operation, and then I went home on a convalescent furlough. When I
returned, the 72nd Squadron had moved from Reading to Knollwood Air
Field near Pinehurst, North Carolina.

The pilots were in the next phase of training — field maneuvers and
hedgehopping missions. They also had practiced landings in outlying
fields in the event we would be forced to land in odd places. After
returning to flying status, I had to fly for several days to get the feel of the
aircraft again.

During this time, a tall, lanky civilian, who had been involved in the
design of the L-5 Sentinel, came from the Stinson factory to teach us some
of the finer points of flying the aircraft. We thought at first that he did not
look very smart, until we watched him take off and handle the aircraft as
if it were an extension of his body.

He showed us how to loop the plane like we had never seen it looped
before. He went up to about 2,000 feet, and then, diving the aircraft, he
pulled up into a loop. However, he did not complete it. Instead, the L-5 just
swiveled into an upright position and took off. He explained later that at
the top of the loop the pilot should lower the flaps to full, causing the plane
to spin on its axis instead of finishing the loop.

He also taught us how to land on a particular spot with a dead engine.
We watched him pass over the field at about 1,000 feet, cut the engine, and
glide in a circle to hit the designated spot every time. He explained that the
pilot should use the flaps as he landed and increase the rate of glide at will,
all the time keeping his eye on the landing spot.

Finally, he taught us the "efficiency takeoff," which wasn't efficient at
all — it was spectacular. This maneuver was performed by, first, on takeoff, picking up speed as the plane rolled down the runway. The aircraft
was to be held on the ground until it reached about 65 miles an hour. Then,
the stick was brought back all the way and the flaps brought to full at the
same time. The aircraft would climb almost straight up for about 200 feet.
Next, the pilot was to ease the stick forward upon approaching stall, then
pick up cruising speed.

After the man from the factory had gone, we practiced his maneuvers enthusiastically. What he had taught us made us all better pilots.

Shortly after I had arrived at Knollwood Field, I lost one of my best friends. Technical Sergeant William Dexter Cleveland had flown into a high electrical line and had been killed instantly. Cleveland and I had gone through liaison training together, as well as through the activation of the squadron. He and I had many beers in many beer joints between Plainview and Knollwood. His death was a jolt to me and enforced a sense of reality in my thinking. I realized what we were doing was a serious matter. Not all of us were going to get out of this war alive.

Although I did not know it at the time, Cleveland had a wife. I met her when she came to get his body. She was a very attractive young lady, but at about 20 years old and already a war widow, she had no real idea how to handle this situation.

Our Public Relations officer took charge when she arrived and escorted her about the field. He helped her make whatever arrangements were necessary to move Cleveland's body back to his home in California. However, the officer was the type of person who would not leave well enough alone. He just had to have some sort of squadron memorial service.

Late in the afternoon he had Cleveland's wife sit in a chair in front of a tent. Knowing that I had been a good friend of her husband and that I knew every pilot in the squadron, he had me stand beside her. He ordered every pilot into formation in front of her. Then each man stepped forward, saluted her, and marched on past. I called out each man's name as he approached her.

When the first men marched toward her and saluted, she began to cry. The men kept coming, and I kept calling names. It went on and on . . . .

Finally, she got herself under control and wiped the tears from her face. She began to giggle. In order to cover up this awkward and seemingly disrespectful act, she tried to make it sound like she was crying. I caught the giggles and could not cover them up, because I was calling out the unending names as the pilots marched past to salute her. Finally the giggles invaded the remaining pilots. As they approached, their faces were contorted into all sorts of stupid shapes. The poor girl finally broke down completely in uncontrollable sobbing. The memorial service finally ended, and Cleveland's poor, young widow had to be helped from her chair and escorted away.

If I could have gotten away with it, I would have boiled that Public Relations officer in oil.

Chapter 4

THE 72ND LIAISON Squadron was scheduled to move from Knollwood Air Field to Skyharbor, Tennessee, an airfield about seven miles east of Nashville. The limited capacity of our fuel tanks required us to make refueling stops at Greenville, North Carolina; Atlanta, Georgia; Birmingham, Alabama; and Lebanon, Tennessee — finally arriving at Skyharbor.

I was assigned to lead the first flight of five L-5s from Knollwood to Greenville. We were the advanced detachment responsible for establishing the camp site. Each aircraft would carry one ground crewman.

For some reason I began to sweat the flight. I had made many cross-country flights, and the terrain over which we were to fly was not bad at all. I studied the maps and drew the flight line. There wasn't anything complicated about it. But, for some unknown reason, I developed a mindset. I was convinced that once I took off and circled the field to pick up the rest of the

The 72nd Liaison Squadron, Skyharbor, Tennessee, 1943.

aircraft, I would fly directly over Pinehurst, the village near Knollwood Field.

That is exactly what I did. For no rhyme or reason, and certainly I have no excuse, I led the flight in a direction that was a good 45 degrees away from the proper route. I had my map lying in my lap, and I began to follow with my eyes the line I had drawn. Obviously I couldn't recognize a landmark.

In about five minutes I was completely lost. I had not the slightest idea where we were. Finally, one of the other pilots flew up under me to the front and waggled his wings. I followed him, and he put us back on course and led us to Greenville. It was one of my most embarrassing moments, but no one said a word. Everyone got lost once in a while. We had a good laugh in Atlanta.

As we pulled up to the flight line that day, a map flew out of the L-5 flown by the Captain leading us. One of the ground crew chased it down, folded it, and brought it back to him, but the Captain refused to touch the soaked map. We would subsequently discover the reason.

There was no relief tube in the L-5, but there was a small ventilator in the fuselage near the right rudder control. The Captain had not been able to wait, so in order to relieve himself he had rolled his map into a tube, placing one end in the ventilator opening, and had done his job. The map had not blown from the cabin, the Captain had thrown it away. And the over-eager ground crewman had returned a badly soiled map to him.

Our advance party, with the help of some Corps of Engineers soldiers, finished readying the encampment at Skyharbor in a relatively short time, and soon the entire 72nd flew in. Our training then took on a more serious tone.

Soon after we had arrived, we began night flight training. Each L-5 had a radio that was of no use because the control tower had no transmitter. The operator used a "biscuit gun" — a very large flashlight-type device — to signal our landings. Normally we came and went off the strip without signals. We just looked very carefully in all directions before taking off and landing.

It was essential that the tower had control over all aircraft. Quadrants were defined in the sky around the airfield. To the northwest of the field, one quadrant was aptly named the "northwest quadrant." The southwest quadrant was another, and so on. Levels were assigned according to altitude: 1,000 feet level, 2,000 feet level, and so on, all around the airfield. Each pilot was assigned a particular level in a particular quadrant.

When training at dusk, we took off about three minutes apart and climbed to our assigned position. On one of these flights I was assigned to the northeast quadrant at 2,000 feet. After we arrived in our quadrant, we flew in circles until we received a green light from the tower. We then entered the traffic pattern, made three landings, and returned to our assigned quadrant. On our last landing, we received a red light and taxied back to the flight line.

Flying in circles at night is a real bore. We flew in the dark for hours, waiting for a green light, and there were many pilots to be steered in for landings. Usually on any given night we only had time for two trips down to the strip. One night, the control operator forgot a pilot circling out there in the darkness. All the others had been called in, but he was left by himself. When he was almost out of fuel, he finally figured out that he had been forgotten, and he came on in to land.

At about this time, our training became more rigorous. Several U.S. Army divisions went on maneuvers a few miles east of Skyharbor. Three of us were sent on Detached Service (DS) to Army headquarters. We took a tent, bed rolls, and cots.

We carried passengers from place to place over the maneuver area, as well as mail and messages. We took off and landed in pastures. The missions we flew were a small-scale introduction to those we would fly for the rest of our Army careers.

It was during this time that I learned the job of a liaison pilot. It certainly was not spotting for the Field Artillery, as we had previously thought. The Army trained its own pilots for that job. Spotters for the artillery were always artillery officers who were gunners first and pilots second. And as far as I know, they flew only Piper Cubs, and really did not consider themselves wartime "pilots" at all.

Winter rains set in at the maneuver area and the weather turned cold. Our tents were frigid. Some nights our cots and blankets were completely inadequate. I tried an experiment one night that should have worked — I would sleep in my winter flying suit.

Made for flight at 30,000 feet, the trousers and coat were sheepskin, with the fleece inside. The attached hood could be pulled over my head and snapped in front of my face. Pullover boots made of sheepskin, also with the wool inside, fit over my regular shoes. No wind could hit me, and I could stay warm at the North Pole.

At first, my idea worked just fine. The suit warmed me up, and I drifted off to sleep easily. However, during the night I awoke stiff and extremely uncomfortable. I wasn't cold, but I was aching in every part of my body. I couldn't go back to sleep. Then I discovered what was wrong. Under blankets a person continually turns, moves, and adjusts his arms and legs. In the winter flying suit, my body could not adjust itself. No matter where I turned, the suit followed me. It did not take long for my body to tire; I felt completely exhausted all the next day. I never tried that experiment again.

We returned to the squadron at Knollwood Air Field at the end of maneuvers. Throughout the months of November and December 1943, we began flying cross-country in earnest. The weather was bad most of the time. We learned to fly by the seat of our pants at 200 feet. No one was ashamed to follow a railroad track, if it led to his destination.

I was weathered-in at Indianapolis for two days and had to sleep in the hangar for two nights. During the day I moped at the door watching the rain. I was away from my squadron, and it was like being away from home.

Finally, another liaison pilot, whom I had never seen before, said he was familiar with the country and that he was going to head out. After talking it over, I learned he was going in my direction and decided I would follow him, hoping the weather had cleared farther south.

When the rain slowed a bit, we took off. The ceiling was not more than 500 feet, and wisps of fog drifted below the clouds toward the ground. I fell in behind him, and we started following a railroad track at an altitude of about 200 feet. When we had flown about 20 minutes, he turned off to the right and disappeared into the wisps of fog. I didn't know whether he had had enough of the weather and was going back to Indianapolis, or if he had come to the place where he was supposed to leave the tracks.

In any case, I was completely lost, except for the railroad track. But I had a full tank of fuel, and thus I followed the track until the weather began to clear. Finally I was able to climb higher, where I could see familiar landmarks. I slept on my own cot in Tennessee that night.

On Christmas Eve 1943, I got weathered in at Bowling Green, Kentucky. It was so bad that I could not go anywhere. Worse, there was no military installation around, and I had to spend the night in a hotel.

On Christmas day I went to the USO and asked where I could get a meal. The lady behind the desk said a Mrs. Travelstead had prepared a Christmas dinner for soldiers. She gave me directions, and I went to the kind lady's home.

Mrs. Travelstead met me at the door. She was a tall woman, about 65 years old, dressed neatly, and had a very dignified appearance. When she invited me in, she smiled as though I were a returning son. She led me to the dining room, in which a large table, very tastefully set, was loaded with food. A large roasted turkey formed the centerpiece.

There was enough food for a banquet but, unfortunately, no one else arrived to share it. She showed me to a chair and brought in some coffee. I began to eat, and she passed me food that I could hardly reach across the large table. I was starving for home-cooked food, and before me was a feast. For dessert she brought out a big slice of apple pie and a fresh cup of coffee.

It must have taken me more than hour to finish that great meal. All during this time no one else came to eat. When I left, I thanked her sincerely. She had given me a special present and made me feel at home. I could not ask for anything more. Her hospitality has remained a pleasant memory.

In late February 1944, we transferred from Skyharbor, Tennessee, to Raleigh-Durham Army Air Base in North Carolina. We flew via Chattanooga, Atlanta, Charlotte, and then to Raleigh-Durham, where we prepared for overseas duty. We did not do much flying, except for special tasks such as several long round-robins, and we practiced picking up messages from ground hooks on our L-5s. We took the required 20-mile hike, we qualified firing the carbine, and we pilots were each issued a .45-caliber automatic pistol with one clip of ammunition.

One day we lined up in single file in front of the medical tent and held out both arms. As we walked past, two medics gave us a full course of shots. Then, one afternoon we were called into formation and marched to a grassy field near headquarters. Our Commanding Officer (CO), Major James S. Percy, told us to stand at ease, following which he told us to sit down and get comfortable. We could smoke if we wanted.

"Well, this is it," he said simply. "Tomorrow we ship out for overseas. We leave here, go by train to Camp Patrick Henry, Virginia, and wait there until transportation is arranged for shipment overseas." He said a few other words, then dismissed us.

The next day we spent packing and getting ready to move out. Early that night we marched from our base to the railroad station in a driving rain. In darkness, marching through the rain to an unknown destination gave us a feeling we will never experience again. I had lost the long view. I could only comprehend what was happening right at that very moment.

We were on our way to war.

Chapter 5

ON APRIL 24, 1944, the 72nd Liaison Squadron arrived at Camp Patrick Henry, Hampton Roads, Virginia, Port of Embarkation (POE). We were to wait for the ship that would take us overseas and deliver us to our fate.

Our train stopped beside a large warehouse platform. Someone we could not see spoke to us over a loudspeaker.

"All troops remain on the train until told to detrain. At that time you will line up facing the warehouse in two columns."

There was a pause, a short silence.

"Detrain," he ordered.

We all silently left the train. There was no speaking or laughter, only the dead rattle of equipment. We stayed on the platform only a moment before we were marched off through a slight mist. The ground was wet from a previous rain, with many puddles along the road.

We heard the deep vibrant tones of an organ from somewhere

in the forest of tall pine trees. It did not particularly matter where the music came from. We were enveloped in the mood it created — a feeling of wonder in all of us as we silently marched along.

Our daily routine while we were at Camp Patrick Henry was very slack. Most of the time we just spent waiting. However, we were not idle. Our equipment was frequently checked for completeness. We attended orientation films. On one occasion we practiced abandoning ship on rope ladders hanging against a wall.

Roll call was held every morning. If there was something to do, we were marched off to the task. Our barracks were checked regularly, but we kept them clean and neat out of habit. A large service club nearby served cold beer, and almost every afternoon several of us went for a few beers at the bar.

We pilots had to fly at least four hours a month in order to qualify for flight pay, which was 50 percent of our base pay. As April passed into May, we needed to fulfill our flight requirement or we would lose considerable money. Some L-5s were brought into the airport at Hampton Roads, and we spent several days away from Camp Henry, while we put in our flying time.

While we waited, the war, in a manner of speaking, caught up with us.

One morning during roll call, we pilots were told to go the barracks and dress in fatigues, leggings, web belts, and helmet liners. We were going on a special detail. We were not told what the detail was, except we were to report to Pier #14, Hampton Roads POE. When we left the barracks, a line of trucks was waiting for us. As the trucks drove to the port, we were informed of our duty.

Two boatloads of German prisoners of war, former soldiers of Field Marshal Erwin Rommel's *Afrika Korps*, had arrived. We were assigned the duty of assisting in their processing after they had disembarked from the ship. Our job was to search the POWs.

When we arrived we were marched into a large, empty warehouse. While still standing at attention we were given a stern lecture by a

Lieutenant we had never seen before. I'm paraphrasing, but this is almost exactly what he said.

"Each of you will be given a paper sack. You will immediately put all your matches, cigarettes, jewelry, watches, money, fountain pens, and cigarette lighters in the paper sacks. You will pick a non-com to be in charge of the paper sacks. When the search is finished your sack will not be returned to you until you have been thoroughly searched by an officer. You will be court-martialed if any German equipment, jewelry, medals, or papers are found on you."

Then, when the search began, the officers stripped the POWs of their valuables. They were harvesting souvenirs!

After we had subsequently searched the POWs, they were lined up in formation against a wall. When a certain number was reached, they were marched away. I found very interesting the fact that almost every one of them carried a picture of Adolf Hitler. I don't recall ever seeing an American soldier carrying a picture of President Franklin Delano Roosevelt.

Our boat sailed from Hampton Roads on June 5, 1944. The next day, D-Day as it was known, the Normandy invasion was launched onto the shores of France. For the first couple of days, rumors had swept the ship. Radio communication on the high seas was extremely limited due to the danger of German U-boats. Finally word was passed down to all decks. The Allies had landed. The second front had successfully been established and was operational.

The pilots of the 72nd Liaison Squadron were appointed as Military Police. This was a break. We wore black arm bands with the initials MP in white. We had full access to the lower, enlisted men's deck and three meals a day, compared with only two meals for the other soldiers; we also had access to the coffee pot. About all we had to do was to walk around, and if we saw anybody sitting on his life belt, we were to tell him to get off. We each had four hours on duty and twelve hours off. With this schedule, we sometimes served duty in the daytime and then later at night.

On the first day out we had discovered a contingent of WACs —

Women's Army Corps — was on board. They were enlisted personnel; however, they were congregated on the upper deck that was reserved for officers. A lot of public necking was going on, all plainly visible from our lower deck. Grumbling among the troops began on the second day.

On the morning of the third day, a voice ringing with authority came over the ship's speaker. My guess was that it was the Captain.

"There will be no fraternizing between officers and enlisted personnel. I repeat, there will be no fraternizing between officers and enlisted personnel. This is an order!" he announced.

The WACs disappeared from the upper decks. I don't know where they went, but they were never seen again.

The ship sailed a southerly route across the Atlantic Ocean. Every seven minutes it made an evasive turn to the right or left, zigzagging to lessen the chance of an attack by German U-boats. One day we passed two dead bodies on a life raft.

On the eighth day at sea we saw our first land — Spanish Morroco. A day later we sailed through the Straits of Gibraltar into the Mediterranean Sea. It was then that we learned our destination was to be North Africa — Oran, Algeria.

From the harbor, Oran sat wedged back into the barren, raw, treeless hills. The flat, sun-baked stucco houses looked ancient and menacing. We disembarked on the docks and loaded into a waiting convoy of trucks. We were driven to a small village a few miles east of Oran named Fleuras. After nine days on a transport, the tents we would live in, seemed luxurious.

On the afternoon of our arrival, a soldier had walked over a small hill near our encampment and had returned with the great news that he had seen a shower installation manned by Italian POWs. There were plenty of showers just waiting to be used.

All of us were absolutely filthy. Some of the fellows could not wait to get into those showers. About ten of them headed over the little hill. I was occupied with something and could not go immediately.

In about 30 minutes the men returned — still dirty. There was indeed a place to shower; however, the water contained so many minerals that soap would not lather. It had gummed up in their hair and had been

Technical Sergeant James R. Bryce on a hill in North Africa, 1944.

impossible to rinse out. They were a messy, miserable bunch of soldiers.

A couple of days later we were taken to another place where we showered and put on clean clothes.

Just a few scrubby trees dotted the barren rolling mounds of landscape around our encampment at Fleuras. The only interesting feature was a hill, or rather a small peak about 1,000 feet high to the north of our camp. In the mornings, if the temperature and humidity were just right, the wind passing over the top would form clouds on the downside of the hill.

After a few days there, with little to do other than stand roll call in the morning, boredom set in. I suggested to a couple of friends that I would like to hike to the top of the hill, and they thought it was a good idea. We asked permission, which was immediately granted.

So one morning we filled our canteen, went by the cook tent to pick up a couple of boxes of K-rations, and set out. The sky was clear and the breeze was still cool.

We had no road to follow, we simply kept the hill in view ahead and made our own path. The ground was scrubby with small trees, weeds, and a few cactus, but hiking was not difficult. As we proceeded along our way we gradually became aware of the old adage, "a hill is always farther away than it looks."

From our encampment, the path to the hill had looked like it would consist only of scrub brush and gullies. Our first hint that there may be more came when we stumbled upon an Arab village with houses built of dried mud and cactus. We were walking through undergrowth of large stands of cactus and were almost in the village before we noticed it. The cactus was a different species from what I was familiar with in Texas. The fronds were much larger and the plants grew in a vine-like manner. The village was not large, and instead of streets, trails wound among the dwellings. The cactus grew up the sides and over the tops of the dried-mud houses.

Little children ran about on the dirt paths that passed between the houses. They stared at us out of curiosity, but they did not beg, as had the other children we had seen in Africa.

A few miles past the Arab village we ran into another surprise — a full-fledged British military base. Dozens of tents were spread out before us.

The British flag flew proudly from a tall pole. Sentries stood guard at the entrance to the compound and stared at us as we walked past. Neither the village nor the camp had been visible from our location. We had thought we were more or less alone in this part of Africa.

The slope up the hill began shortly beyond the British camp. The climb was not very difficult because of the mountain's gradual incline. About noon we arrived at the top. We looked out across the blue Mediterranean and tried to imagine that we could see the coast of Spain. Almost 1,000 feet below was a deserted beach. About three miles to the west, just off the beach, was the hull of a ship that must have been sunk in some recent engagement.

Farther west, in the distance, was Oran and its harbor. To the south, for miles, we could see rolling plains, little villages here and there, winding roads, well laid-out grape racks, and a few depressions that looked like dry lakes.

We arrived back at our camp late in the afternoon.

While at Fleuras we received one pass into Oran. Our trucks dropped us off in a city park about 9 a.m. on the morning of a beautiful day. We spread out into the side streets leading from the park. As we wandered around, staring at the strange sights, we heard a trumpet playing very good American Dixieland jazz. Caught by surprise, we followed the sound of the music into a building, crowded with soldiers, mostly British and French.

Our little group worked its way to the bar and ordered some drinks. We were served beer in tin cans. Those who ordered whiskey were served in small shot glasses made from the tops of Coca-Cola bottles that had been cut in two where the mouthpiece joined the neck. This segment had been turned over, plugged, and placed on a small wood base so that it could stand upright. I did not see a normal shot glass, beer bottle, or beer mug along the entire bar. The beer was served at room temperature.

While in the bar, a new experience provided me with one of the biggest laughs I had during my war years. When I first entered the men's restroom, it looked like any other. On the right side was a row of urinals attached to the walls. On the left was a row of stalls for commodes. All the urinals were being used when I walked in, so I opened the door to one of the stalls. But no commode was inside, only a round hole in the middle of the floor.

Perhaps a shower stall, I thought. I looked into another stall and saw the same thing. I was confused and started to open another door. Then I noticed one of my acquaintances leaning against one of the doors. He was choked with laughter. He opened the door to the stall and pointed to the hole in the floor. I had not noticed before that on each side of the hole was a raised place, the shape of a man's shoe. I could not believe it. These people did not use commodes. They squatted over a hole.

We stayed in North Africa a little less than a month. We had learned that we were heading to Italy. Our second ship was too small and smelled bad, and must have been a luxury liner on the Far East run during Queen Victoria's reign during the 19th century.

Chapter 6

THREE DAYS LATER, as we sailed into Naples harbor, we stood at the rail and marveled at the sights. Ahead, Mount Vesuvius loomed as a backdrop for the city. The Isle of Capri was on the left of the harbor entrance. To the right, forming the southern curve of the bay, was Sorrento, the city that had inspired the romantic song, "Come Back to Sorrento."

The harbor was crowded with assorted ships from many nations. Ours carefully worked its way toward the docks and pulled alongside a capsized hulk that had been sunk in an earlier engagement. We marched down a plank bridge and walked to the pier on its hull.

As we stepped ashore, an Italian civilian drove by on the street in a beat-up old Italian truck, singing at the top of his voice, "O Sole Mio," the old Neopolitan street song. What a memorable moment for me! Welcome to Italy!

We were loaded into trucks at the pier and driven north through

Naples several miles to Caserta, where we camped in tents near two long earthen runways of the Santa Maria Airport. Four of us could share and not be crowded in the large tent. The floors were wood and the sides could be rolled up to allow plenty of ventilation.

We were told that our L-5s, which had been crated for shipment, were on the docks. After the mechanics arrived, they would assemble and deliver the aircraft to us in a few days. This meant we had a few days to loaf around our encampment and explore our surroundings. The airport and our camp were surrounded by large fields of flax, a tall, slender, and reed-like plant that grows almost six feet high. They were grown so close together that they formed an almost impenetrable wall on either side of the access rows.

Nearby, we discovered a field of ripe corn. We rounded up some large cans and some salt. We built a fire next to the field, and started water boiling in the cans. When the corn was ready, we threw in some salt and put in several ears to boil. The treat was delicious. For a few nights we had regular picnics. We never heard a word from the farmer or anyone else.

One afternoon as I was reading on my cot, with the sides of the tent rolled up and a comfortable breeze blowing through, I noticed a civilian walk by and approach the flax field behind my tent. Civilians normally steered clear of a military installation unless they had business there. I watched this person to see what he was up to.

He began to knock a path through the tall flax. He soon disappeared, but I could hear his progress through the field. Shortly, he returned from the path he had made through the flax and left the premises. He then returned with a girl, about 20 years old, who was carrying a blanket. They both disappeared along the path. He returned and stood silently at its entrance. It did not take the deductive powers of a Sherlock Holmes to figure out what was going on.

Soon, two soldiers from our squadron showed up, each handing the man a can of food. He placed the food in a bag. One of the men went down the path, and in about five minutes he returned. Then the other man disappeared into the flax.

In about five minutes the second man returned, and the two soldiers left. It was not long until a parade of soldiers was passing my tent. The man's

bag was rapidly filling up with canned goods. I did not see one pilot in the line.

Late in the afternoon a soldier ran up to the line of men and whispered something to one of the soldiers. Like lightning the word spread, and the soldiers scattered. The man with the bag of goods yelled at the girl. She appeared at the entrance to the path, carrying the blanket. Both took off at a dead run.

In five minutes the MPs arrived, they entered the path, and rummaged around in the flax. They asked every one around our tents if a prostitute had been working the area. No one, including me, had seen a thing. The MPs left and the matter was closed.

No doubt some poor Italians had a square meal that night.

When we received our aircraft, we were ready to fly again after the long break. The first plane completed went to Major Percy, our Commanding Officer. We all gathered by the runway to watch the Major test-hop his new aircraft. As he gathered speed on the runway and lifted off into flight, we cheered as if he had just run 100 yards for a touchdown.

On July 22, 1944, my L-5 was ready, and I took off for a test-hop. I felt rusty at the controls, but after several landings, I left the airfield and roamed over the countryside at about 2,000 feet.

The Italian terrain was different from what I was used to in the States. There were fewer roads, smaller fields, and clearly defined villages. When I flew over a small village, the outskirts did not gradually fade out along a road or into outlying suburbs. Villages had clearly defined boundaries that stopped directly at the edge of outlying fields or vineyards. One village sat on top of a hill, covering it like a cap. Its edges stopped abruptly just below the crown of the hill. The dirt road leading from the village wound down the side of the hill in a serpentine manner.

I flew three and a half hours, until I was almost out of fuel. Upon my return, I taxied to the flight line and was met by the mechanic assigned to my aircraft.

"How was it?" he asked.

"It flies!" I replied.

The assembly and testing of my aircraft ended on that ritual. I was ready to go to work.

The 72nd Liaison Squadron was attached to the Seventh Army Head-quarters located at Caserta. We were at the hub of almost all military operations in southern Italy. As a result, we carried military personnel with business at headquarters from south of Naples to the front lines, located north of Rome. Every pilot in the squadron was put into continual service.

Many flights were so repetitive that they turned into milk runs. One such flight was from Caserta to Castellabate, a small village located on a rocky point of land south of Naples called P. Lacosa. Each time I carried a passenger on this flight we flew over Mount Vesuvius. I would circle over the crater several times so my passenger could get a good look into it. The sides of the cone went almost straight down. The bottom was not flat, but rather lumpy and mostly covered with yellowish sulphur. Smoke rose from several places.

After viewing the volcano, we flew across the Bay of Naples and circled the Isle of Capri, a vacation spot for the rich since Roman times. Very elaborate villas could be seen from the air, and there was a small village just above the docks.

I flew my passenger on to Sorrento on the slope of the peninsula bordering the south end of Bay of Naples. I followed the coast to Salerno where the Allies had landed during the invasion of Italy. Several marble pillars, the remains of the ancient Roman town, Paestum, rose above the sands near the beach. We finished our tour upon landing at Castellabate.

I feel sure to this day the persons I had carried on this milk run remember it well. Although I made the trip many times, each time I was very impressed.

So many missions were being flown to Castellabate that it was finally decided to send a pilot on Detached Service to the U.S. Army unit stationed there. On August 1, 1944, I was temporarily attached to the 1st Special Services Forces under the command of Colonel (soon to be General) Robert T. Frederick at Castellabate. The town is so small it is not shown on many maps. There is no beach between the village and the sea. The gentle waves of the Mediterranean break against the rocks on which some of the buildings stand. On the north edge of Castellabate, Colonel Frederick established his headquarters in a villa. The two-storied building looked like a pink cube. Except for some terra cotta designs around the doors and windows, it was plain.

When I arrived at Castellabate, I placed my cot and bed roll in a bare room on the second floor of a small building facing the only street that ran through the little village. Standing at the window of the room I could look out on a narrow, cobblestone street that probably had felt the tread of Roman soldiers passing that way long, long ago. Very little traffic was seen other than the local citizens going about their business.

I have forgotten the name of the soldier that shared my room. He was the driver for Colonel Frederick and had been with him at Anzio, the Allied beachhead north of Rome. Every soldier at Anzio had been caught between the German artillery and the sea for months. It had been murderous duty. British Prime Minister Winston S. Churchill had referred to Anzio as the Allies' "beached whale."

My roommate had been on Anzio for months, and he exhibited the same characteristics I noted many times later in men who had been under heavy enemy fire. It may have been his regular personality, but on the other hand it may have been generated out of a long period of fright. He was very up-tight, nervous, and fidgety. He had been through hell. He knew something was being planned there in Castellabate, and he knew he was going to have to drive the Colonel back into the fight.

The driver was taking sulpha drugs that he had gotten from a medic. The medication must have been murder on his body. He told me he was having relations with several Italian girls in Castellabate, and that he took the drugs as a pre-emptive strike against venereal disease. I thought it was more dangerous for him to be soaking his body with sulpha drugs than facing German artillery.

I was kept very busy flying every day. Colonel Frederick's staff officers had a lot of business in Naples. The morning flight from Castellabate to Capodichino Airport in Naples became a milk run. But on the morning of August 5, 1944, it turned out to be quite different. My passenger was wearing two stars on his collar, and looked to be about 45 or 50 years old. I knew for sure he was not one of Colonel Frederick's staff officers.

As he approached, I snapped to attention and saluted. He returned my salute and climbed into the aircraft without saying a word. He looked like a man with lots on his mind. The flight to Capodichino was uneventful. When we landed, I followed him — two steps in the rear and keeping in pace with him — to his waiting car near the ready room. As we walked, my curiosity got the best of me.

"Sir," I said, with deepest respect. "I'll need your name for my log book."

"It's Patch. A. M. Patch," he replied. It was the only thing he said during the entire flight. Major General Alexander M. Patch (soon to be Lieutenant General) was the Commanding General of the Seventh Army.

A low but rather steep hill rose to the north of Castellabate, about two miles from the landing strip at Colonel Frederick's headquarters. The hill ran from a mountain several miles off to the right, westward the length of the peninsula, where it sloped into the sea. Because its elevation did not cause any problem, I usually climbed right over it after takeoff. On other occasions I would fly out over the sea around the promontory just because the scenery was better.

One morning I was to take a staff officer, whose name I do not recall, to Capodichino. He was waiting for me at the landing strip when I arrived. He was carrying a camera and asked if I would mind taking him over Paestum, the old Roman city, so that he could take some photos. This caused no problem. Paestum was near Salerno, which was on a long beach north of Castellabate.

I chose to fly over the hill because of a strong north wind. As I approached, the ride was very smooth. I had not the slightest warning of what was about to happen. I suddenly lost control of the aircraft and crashed into the side of the hill. I had flown into the turbulence caused by the down-draft of the wind coming down over the crest of the hill. Neither I nor my passenger were scratched, but the aircraft was completely demolished.

Later that day one of my squadron mates arrived to pick me up and return me to Santa Maria Airport at Caserta. In a few days I had a brand-new aircraft. Battle plans were changing, and we were preparing to move out.

On August 16, 1944, about half of us pilots left Caserta and flew north to the little coastal village of Piombino, off of which lay the island of Elba, where Napoleon Bonaparte had been exiled in 1814, after his earlier defeat in Russia.

Chapter 7

AT PIOMBINO, we learned that we were to take part in the invasion of southern France. The day before we had arrived, August 15, 1944, American and French amphibious forces had begun OPERATION DRAGOON, under the command of Lieutenant General Alexander M. Patch, who had been promoted since August 5th, when I flew him from Castellabate to Capodichino.

Our aircraft were lined up along the south side of the long, dirt runway. All day long we watched a wing of Republic P-47 Thunderbolts take off, return, refuel, reload, and take off again on their bombing and strafing missions in support of OPERATION DRAGOON.

One day, about the middle of the afternoon, a group of us were lounging near the edge of the runway as a flight of P-47s returned from a mission. Customarily, the flight composed of about ten aircraft came over the field in echelon formation. After making their pass each would then, in turn, peel off, circle the field, and land. Thus, the aircraft were properly separated on their approach to the runway.

As we watched, two approaching P-47s came in too close to each other. We could see the accident coming before it happened. One aircraft landed on top of the other. As the top aircraft hit, the landing gear on the bottom one crumbled, and both planes dug up a cloud of dirt. It sounded like the crushing of a thousand tin cans. Then out of the noise and cloud of dirt flew the body of the pilot of the bottom aircraft. Before he hit the ground, 50 feet in front of the crashing P-47, we could tell he was dead. The runway was wide enough for the other aircraft to land safely beside the wreckage.

We had no idea when we would leave Piombino, but idleness did not hang heavy. We knew what was going on in France, and we did not really feel in a hurry to get there. At night we usually built a fire and roasted weenies, or just went to our bedrolls and tried to get plenty of sleep. We had no opportunity to go into town, so we did not have any refreshments to drink.

A Sergeant in our Operations section there was very repulsive. When he played poker he got drunk and made every one mad. He was just plain mean. No one liked him. In addition, the Sergeant had a bad habit. When someone was eating a candy bar or something, he would sneak up, grab the food, and cram it into his mouth. He was really annoying. I swore to myself that if he ever did that to me, I would nail him.

One night we built a fire and were toasting slices of bread stuck to the end of a stick. I was holding my bread over the fire when the Sergeant made his move. He sneaked up behind me, grabbed the piece off my stick, crammed it into his mouth, jumped over the fire, and took off.

I went after him in a dead run. When I caught him, I jumped on his shoulders and pushed him to the ground. I had my hand on the back of his head, and when we hit the ground we skidded a few feet on the gravel. I mashed his face into the ground with all my weight. Then I turned his head over and forced my finger into his mouth and pulled the bread out and smeared the mess all over his face.

I returned to the fire and left him standing on the outskirts of the fire.

"I didn't think you'd get mad," he said, in a weak voice.

As far as I know, he never grabbed anything from anyone else after that night.

On August 24, 1944, we left Piombino and flew across the Ligurian Sea to southern France. This was to be a long flight across open sea, so we landed at Bastia, Corsica, to top off our tanks before heading toward our destination.

About ten aircraft were in the group, and we flew in a loose echelon. The remaining pilots in the 72nd Squadron had stayed behind at Caserta's Santa Maria Airport, continuing to fly missions in Italy. Later, they would be transported to France by ship. The flight in an L-5 took more than five hours, including the stopover at Bastia, and should have been scary. For almost the entire trip we were out of sight of land. The flight stretched the limit of our fuel capacity, and we had to hit a narrow beachhead surrounded by Germans.

But I was not worried in the least. We flew at about 3,000 feet. The person responsible for navigating us to our goal was one of our officers, whose job it was to get us there. It was his job to sweat.

I had a mechanic in the back seat, and our duffle bags and personal gear were stacked all around him. He sat back and watched the ocean roll by. I found out later he was scared to death.

Late in the afternoon, I began to look for land. I first saw the clay-red French soil off to my right. As we came closer, I began to see the small white villas. I began to see Allied ships and barges ahead. Finally, I could make out American landing craft and other small U.S. vessels along the beach. Then I saw the barrage balloons, suspended from cables attached to ships and barges. The balloons were to protect the vessels from strafing by enemy aircraft.

Our leader waggled his wings to signal us to tighten our echelon. Then he turned us to the right, away from the barrage balloons. We flew ashore east of the landing craft and continued inland. I did not realize it at the time, but we had flown over the French Riviera, one of the most desirable pieces of real estate in the world. There was little war damage to the buildings, but there was plenty of damaged bridges, roads, and railheads.

A few miles inland we came to a village called Brignoles. Our leader led us in a circle over a level green, grass-covered field that looked like a

↯ From Darmstadt, Germany, last flight in L-5 to Army Depot in Creil, France, June 20, 1945.

★ The 72nd Liaison Squadron flew from Piombino, Italy, to Brignoles, France, August 24, 1944.

well-kept lawn, just south of the town. As we landed we were directed to one side of the strip where our aircraft were lined up in a row. Major Percy, our CO, came out to each aircraft and shook the pilot's hand.

"Well done," he said. "I'm glad to see you."

I believe he was really glad we had made it.

As I unbuckled my parachute harness, my mechanic, who had been silent since we had left Italy, reached forward and tapped me on the shoulder. "Your shaving kit fell out of the airplane," he said.

"What!" I replied, remembering distinctly placing my kit behind his head. "How did it happen?"

"When you were circling to get into formation over Piombino it fell out past my head when you were banking."

I had been flying with my windows open.

"Why didn't you tell me?"

"I figured you had enough on your mind."

I could tell he was really glad to get out of the aircraft and step again onto solid ground.

I had arrived in France on August 24, 1944, and immediately began drawing combat pay. We quickly learned that we could exercise a freedom we had never anticipated. We landed rather late in the afternoon, and someone asked if we could walk into Brignoles about a half a mile away. We were informed that we could go anywhere we wanted, as long as we were ready to fly when we were called upon and we did what we were told to do. It was a rule that held for the duration of the war.

While in Brignoles we flew constantly. We carried personnel, mail, documents, and sometimes small cargo all over the Riviera within the perimeter of the expanding front. To the west of us, the main German force was in full retreat up the Rhone Valley north of Marseilles. The invasion — OPERATION DRAGOON — had been an outstanding success. The Seventh Army under General Patch was in bloody pursuit.

The high quality of American military leadership had revealed itself many times during DRAGOON. One such example occurred shortly after we had arrived in Brignoles.

The American Army's Task Force Butler was advancing north toward Grenoble. Lieutenant General Lucien K. Truscott, Commander of the

United States VI Corps, set a trap. In a monumental tactical move, he ordered the Task Force to cross the mountains between Brignoles and Grenoble and intercept the retreating Germans. With the help of the Free French of the Interior (FFI), also called the *Maqui* — a militia organized by General Charles DeGaulle, who had fought the Germans in the mountains as partisans — the Task Force arrived at the Rhone River ahead of the Germans, effectively cutting off their retreat.

The slaughter was terrible. The Task Force stalled German retreat long enough for P-47s to be called in to strafe the columns of German soldiers. American artillery, operating from the high ground, pounded them continously.

Several of our liaison pilots flew personnel to the site of the slaughter, and along the roads around Montélimar. These pilots reported seeing dead bodies everywhere. Dead horses littered the countryside. Destroyed German tanks, artillery pieces, and trucks were scattered all over the area.

I did not go look. I could imagine the devastation. I began to realize that war was an unforgiving business. Many people had been killed and more would lose their lives.

Because of the rapidity of the German retreat, our stay at Brignoles did not last long. On our last day I was assigned to Detached Service at Grenoble. The squadron was to move ahead to Lons-le-Saunier, which was well north of Grenoble.

My last flight out of Brignoles on September 3, 1944, was a character builder. It was my turn to make the mail run from Brignoles to St. Raphaël to Grasse and back to Brignoles. Mail bags were loaded into my L-5's back seat and tied down, then I took off.

I had heard of the problem at St. Raphaël. Pilots who had made the run before had mentioned that the landing strip was on a golf course fairway running northwest and sloping toward the southeast. When I arrived, I noticed the wind was pretty strong out of the northwest, but I had little trouble landing into it at the bottom of the sloping runway.

A courier was waiting for the mail, and he loaded some bags aboard my aircraft. The exchange took no more than five minutes, and I was ready to take off for Grasse.

I knew immediately I was going to have a problem getting the aircraft back off the ground. The northwest end of the strip, where I had unloaded the mail, was not only the high end, but was also bordered by tall trees and a power line. However, in order to take off into the northwest wind, I would have to start my run at the southeast end to clear everything.

When in doubt, take off into the wind. I taxied my aircraft to the southeast end. I climbed out of the cockpit, then lifted the tail of the L-5 and dragged it back off the end of the strip as far as I could. I wanted all the distance possible. When I got back in the aircraft and looked ahead up that slope toward those trees and that power line, I felt very scared. I did not see how I could possibly get over those obstacles.

Nevertheless, pulling down full flaps, I pushed the throttle forward, and started rolling. The L-5 just could not get enough speed going uphill. The controls would not take hold, and I knew I was not going to make it. Hitting the brakes, I almost nosed the aircraft over. I noticed the courier who had picked up the mail was sitting in his Jeep watching me.

I studied the idea of taking off downwind, down the sloping strip. There were no trees or obstacles at the other end and the ground sloped only slightly beyond. Again, I climbed the aircraft and pulled the tail back as far as I could. This time, when I pushed the throttle forward, I held the brakes until the tail was almost off the ground. Then I let off the brakes and started to roll. The L-5 would not break free. The tailwind was pushing too hard for the aircraft to achieve enough air speed to lift off. The controls never responded. I braked and almost nosed over again.

My third try would have to be make or break. Again, I pulled the tail back as far as I could. When I got back into the L-5 I looked at those towering trees and the power lines. I saw several soldiers and a few civilians lining the fence row, no doubt waiting to see if I would crash.

I pulled down full flaps and pushed the throttle forward to the stop. Then I took my hand off the throttle and placed it in my lap. I was scared, but I knew it was now or never. As the aircraft rolled forward, I felt the controls begin to respond to the air. I pulled back on the stick, but I felt it get mushy; I eased off as it gained resistance. As the plane lifted, I continued to pull back the stick, climbing into a near stall. As the trees and power lines approached, I felt a lift, the stick tightened up, and an up-draft took me over the top of the trees and the lines. I looked down to see the obstacles hardly more than three feet below my wheels.

The soldiers and civilians were waving wildly at me. I just shook my head. That was one close call.

My landing at Grasse was uneventful, except when I hit the ground a tire blew out. I taxied the L-5 to the Operations tent, where I was met by a courier and a mechanic. While the courier unloaded mail sacks and placed others in the back seat, the mechanic went into a maintenance tent. He returned with another tire and replaced my flat one.

When the mechanic later examined the flat tire, he found that in my braking at St. Raphaël, the friction from one of the brakes had burned through the inner tube.

I returned to Brignoles, and this should be the end of that particular story. But not quite. . . .

When I landed, an officer and a liaison pilot approached my L-5. The field was deserted, because the rest of the 72nd Liaison Squadron had moved out for Lons-le-Saunier.

"I've got one more mail run for St. Raphaël and Grasse," he said. "One of you has to take it."

I told him I was going to Grenoble.

"You can go on to Grenoble from Grasse," he said. "One of you guys has to take it."

I did not want to try to get my aircraft off the ground again at St. Raphaël. When both of us pilots hesitated, the officer did not blink an eye. He reached into his pocket and pulled out a coin.

"One of you call it," he ordered, and flipped the coin into the air.

"Heads," I said.

It came up heads. The other pilot walked off to his aircraft.

I climbed into mine and headed for Grenoble.

Would I have gone back to St. Raphaël? Of course, I would; I was in the Army. But I sure wouldn't *volunteer* to go through that experience again.

Chapter 8

ON SEPTEMBER 4, 1944, I flew from Brignoles to Grenoble. I landed at a small municipal airport south of town, that had one hangar. The Germans had driven large spikes into the ground all over the runway so that an aircraft could not land, but our Infantry, or some unit, had removed enough of them so that we could use the field. I put my cot and bedroll in the hangar. A small detachment of personnel on some other mission was already there, so we were well supplied with food.

I had arrived early in the afternoon. Grenoble is located in the French Alps. The weather was turning from balmy, spring-like conditions on the Riviera to the early winter mists of the mountains. A slight rain began to fall, and I knew I was not going to fly any more that day.

I caught a jeep into town to look around. Hardly touched by war damage, Grenoble had the appearance I had always imagined of a French town. The streets were broad and clean and the buildings attractive. Although several sidewalk cafés were open, there were no patrons. Hardly any traffic appeared on the streets.

I felt almost alone. I found a café with sidewalk tables under a marquee, and sat down. All the other tables were vacant. A waiter came out of the restaurant and approached me. He could speak a little English, and I was able to order a glass of wine.

By then, it was getting dark and a light rain provided a steady drip of water from the marquee. I began to feel "Hemingwayesque." There I was, a soldier, sipping wine at a sidewalk café in a French town, with the slow rain creating an atmosphere of mystery. Only a day or so earlier, German soldiers had been in the town, but now they were on the run someplace to the north.

The next day the weather turned bad, but not before my good friend Staff Sergeant James T. Wall showed up. He also had been assigned Detached Service to Grenoble. He had been a very close friend for a long time, and I felt his arrival was a lucky break for me.

The weather remained bad. About the middle of the afternoon we decided to go into Grenoble. We were walking in a park when we saw two very attractive women coming in our direction. We could not speak a word of French, and they could not speak English, but we managed to flirt with them. They returned our greeting and motioned for us to follow. I took the arm of one, and Wall took the other. They escorted us to their apartment.

The women were very well dressed and groomed and seemed educated and cultured. They served us wine, and we spent a very delightful evening trying to speak each other's language.

For the next two days, we could not fly due to rain. But late in the afternoon of each day we gathered some food from our larder in the hangar, then went to the ladies' apartment in Grenoble. They opened the rations and set a beautiful table with the GI food.

One afternoon I was standing at the hangar waiting for a flight. I had not been told who my passenger would be, but I was rarely told anyway. In this case I was surprised I was even allowed to carry the officer. A single jeep pulled up and Lieutenant General Jacob L. Devers, Commander of the Sixth Army Group, stepped out. He outranked General Alexander M. Patch and French General Jean de Lattre de Tassigny. As Commander over the entire Mediterranean Zone of Operations, he reported directly to General Dwight D. Eisenhower, Supreme Allied Commander in the European Theater of War.

Generals normally were accompanied by a bevy of armed guards, but General Devers approached alone. I snapped to attention and gave him my best salute. He saluted me and then extended his hand, which I shook, receiving a firm handshake in return.

"What's your name, Sergeant?" he asked. I told him.

"Where you from?"

"Texas, Sir."

"A good state," he said.

He reached down, placed his thumbs inside his belt, and adjusted his trousers.

"This belt — I don't like it," he said.

The belt was a beautiful, dark-brown leather. The round buckle was engraved with the great seal of the United States.

"The General Staff sent these to all Generals and told us to wear them," he explained. Then he turned and got into the L-5, fastened his parachute harness, and connected his seat belt, telling me, "Let's go," as he closed his window.

I took off and carried him to Ambérieu.

On our last night in Grenoble, Sergeant Wall and I had a fine meal with our two friends. The next morning we were to rejoin our squadron at Lons-le-Saunier.

By the time the 72nd Liaison Squadron had arrived, the invasion forces moving up from southern France had joined the American forces from the north. OPERATION DRAGOON had proven a great military success. The Allied forces were formed into one front line across France, from the North Sea to Switzerland, with the British on the north, the Americans in the center, and the French on the south.

Flying weather worsened as Autumn of 1944 approached, but that did not cut down on our time in the air very much. We had no weather reports of any kind. If we could get an L-5 off the ground, we were told to take off. We were to return if conditions became threatening.

At Lons-le-Saunier, I received the news that my very good friend, Staff Sergeant Harry Clay, had been killed. He was part of the contingent that had remained in Italy. His aircraft had crashed, and he died instantly. He had been buried at a military cemetery at the base of Mount Vesuvius.

Harry and I had been together during our early pilot training at Plainview. We both had been present at the activation of the 72nd Liaison Squadron in New Cumberland, and we had shared a lot of beer together. He was my second close friend to pack it in.

When I heard that Harry was dead, I sat down and tried to figure it all out. I couldn't then, and I can't now.

I also learned that another very good friend of mine, Staff Sergeant Lewis Baker, was missing. He had taken off from Brignoles, carrying a member of the FFI into the mountains northwest of the village. That's the last he had been heard from.

The American Army's supply lines were stretching from the port at Marseilles to the front line that was moving daily around Switzerland toward Germany. I took personnel on the long flight to Marseilles on two occasions. A trip that distance in a L-5, with unpredictable weather, required a little planning. However, on my first trip the weather looked good, so I flew directly to Marseilles, landing on a race track on the south side of town. My passenger told me he would ride back with the convoy he was to assemble. I was to fly back alone.

It was early afternoon; clouds had moved in and rain was lightly falling. Returning that day was out of the question, so I caught a truck and went in to explore Marseilles. As chance would have it, General Charles de Gaulle was there. The town had been liberated almost two weeks, and the streets were filled with wildly happy Frenchmen. Allied flags hung from every window, large crowds were at the entrances to all theaters, and the bars and cafés were open.

The streets were wide and lined with trees, but were so crowded that we moved at a snail's pace. The crowd flowed away from our truck as we passed, like water at the bow of a boat. Many of the Frenchmen stuck out their hands, and I shook hands with them as we rode by.

There was perfume in the air, and the aura of unrestrained joy abounded. I experienced a great pleasure to be among those people and absorb the atmosphere. It seemed that since the Liberation, a great load had been lifted and they were free to continue their lives.

I had an interesting little experience of no consequence in Marseilles. The movie *Snow White and the Seven Dwarfs* was being shown in a little theater on a side street. I decided to see it. Many people smoked, and their smoke rose into the light from the projection booth, creating a haze throughout the crowded theater. The dialogue was dubbed in French. What interested me mostly, however, was that the names of the seven dwarfs, which were carved into the foot of their beds, was in French.

The next day when I was to return to Lons-le-Saunier, I faced very unsettled weather. Instead of going back over the mountains, the way I had come, I decided to follow the Rhone River to Lyon, then cut eastward to Lons-le-Saunier. This I did, and returned without incident.

Two days later, September 18, 1944, I was ordered to fly a Captain who had some business to conduct at Marseilles. This time the weather looked bad when I took off from Lons-le-Saunier. I knew that I had better go by way of Lyon and follow the Rhone River south to the coast. The weather to Lyon was bad, but I could still fly high enough that navigating the distance was no problem. However, when I turned south and began following the Rhone, the weather got progressively worse. The clouds became lower and lower, until I was flying about 300 feet above the river.

I passed an airfield off to my left. I knew, if worse came to worse, I could fly back there and land. About 20 minutes later, I saw ahead of me a solid wall of rain. There was no way I could fly through that, so I decided to turn around and land at the airport I had seen earlier.

Returning up the river, I cut away toward the airport and circled to land. No way. The runways had been rendered useless by carefully placed demolition bombs. A row of French fighter planes, with their engines destroyed by the retreating Germans, were an obstacle as well. I could not put down. There was no way I could get past the rain either, so I returned to Lyon. I gassed up and watched the weather.

The Captain, my passenger, had not said anything as I worked my way through this problem, but while we were still on the ground at Lyon, he spoke. "I don't want to say anything that would affect your judgment, but

I've got to get to Marseilles if at all possible. There's a load of walkie-talkies on the dock, and I've got to get them to the front. They're very short of them."

I told him I would do my best. The weather did not get any better, but I took off anyway and started down the Rhone River once again. I flew about 200 feet above the water. I had made it beyond the airfield where I had hoped to land earlier when I saw another wall of rain. As I approached it, I descended until I was about 100 feet above the water. Then I saw a bomber approaching in my direction, and I veered off to the left. As the bomber passed, I saw it was a British Avro Lancaster. I could plainly see the faces of both the pilot and the co-pilot. They were following the river just as I was, except they were flying in the opposite direction.

As I neared the wall of rain, I saw that it was moving to my left. To the right, the rain was clearing, and I flew in that direction, though I did not want to leave the river, for fear I would be in serious trouble flying in the hills that bordered it. When I had finally flown around the rain, the ceiling began to rise, and I ascended without getting into the clouds. Finally I broke out above a broad coastal plain. The bad weather was behind me, and I climbed higher and higher. I wanted some space to fly in.

Suddenly I heard a loud whooshing sound. A B-25 bomber came up from underneath me, directly in front, going away at enormous speed. It scared the living daylights out of me. I do not know to this day if the pilot almost hit me from behind or was just buzzing me.

I landed on the same race track at Marseilles where I had landed a couple of days earlier. It had been one tough flight! I had been told when I had left on the flight that upon my return I was to fly to Vesoul. The 72nd Liaison Squadron was moving up while I would be away.

Chapter 9

WE WERE THE only pilots using Vesoul's municipal airport. The facility was large and smooth, and the approaches were free of obstruction in all directions. We took pleasure in flying in and out, because it reminded us of an American airport, except that the runways were dirt.

Our tents, on a small hill about a mile east of the airport, were lined up next to a forest. One day I went out into the woods to look around and explore a bit. I could tell there had been a fire fight in the woods recently. A lot of tree branches had been knocked off, and there were shell holes all over where grenades had exploded.

I found a wooden box from the Red Cross that had been blown open. Inside, undamaged, were a bunch of books. There was no telling how they had turned up in the middle of a battle zone. In any case, whoever had packed them had good taste in literature.

I looked through the books and picked one containing a selection of short stories by Guy de Maupassant. I had heard of the author but never had had an opportunity to read any of his work. I took the book back to my tent and read his entertaining stories with deep interest — "The Necklace," "Ball of Fat," and "The Piece of String." The man could really write. He was the clearest writer I believe I have ever read. He could almost make you cry, then jolt you right out of your seat. If I had not found that box of books I would have missed one of life's pleasures.

We received our first taste of German firepower close up in Vesoul. We had an antiaircraft battery near our airfield that had little to do during the day. German aircraft were flying elsewhere. But at night the Germans sent over observation planes. When we heard the sound of the aircraft, and then the *boom, boom, boom*, of the ack-ack gun firing, everyone stood outside his tent and looked skyward, trying to see the action — everyone, that is, except me. As the bullets from our ack-ack guns exploded in the air, the metal fell back to earth. I knew the pieces had to hit someplace.

Each night when the show started, I went outside and crawled under a jeep. That put lots of metal between me and any falling steel shards coming my way. It seemed sensible. I took a lot of kidding about being scared. But one night while I was safe under my jeep, a piece of steel ricocheted off a truck and went whizzing near one fellow's head. I was almost crowded out from under my safe position. I was never kidded about the matter again.

We all had been warned about being strafed by German fighters. It was suggested we each dig a foxhole beside the entrance of our tent. I thought it was a good idea, so I dug mine just outside. I took a lot of kidding about my foxhole, too. I found trash in it occasionally, but always cleaned it out. One day I found someone had defecated in the hole. I didn't clean that out. Things rocked along for a few days, then we were strafed.

The German aircraft came in low and was on top of us before we knew it. Everyone ran in all directions except me. I dove right into my foxhole. But someone had jumped in there first — one of the officers who had kidded me about it. I knew what to do. I landed full on his back and mashed him down, as hard as I could, into the mess.

After the strafing was over and he crawled out, he was a sorry sight. And he couldn't say a word. After all, it was my foxhole. No one kidded me after that.

We received some good news while we were at Vesoul. Staff Sergeant Harold S. Baker had turned up alive, and he had an amazing story to tell. Baker had carried his passenger, an FFI man, into the mountains northwest of Brignoles to a small village. The man was part of a group of partisans operating in the south of France. Baker and his passenger thought the village had been cleared of Germans, and thus he landed his plane in the square. However, the Germans still occupied one side. When Baker rolled to a stop, the Germans fired on them with machine guns. Baker and his passenger managed to escape to the other side of the square, but his aircraft had been destroyed.

Baker stayed with the partisans until they left the region. Then they took him safely to some Americans, who returned him to the 72nd Liaison Squadron.

On September 29, 1944, I flew to Verdun. The town and the surrounding countryside had been the site of some of the most vicious fighting during World War I. Thousands of men had lost their lives there. I was surprised to still see miles and miles of World War I trenches. None were straight, but zigzagged across the countryside. I had assumed they would have been filled in, eroded away, or plowed up for farm land by that time.

One of our pilots flew General Patch over the trenches. Patch pointed out the ones he had fought in. Surely there is a lesson here that should be learned. Something is wrong when two disasters, the magnitude of World War I and World War II, occurred within less than three decades of each other — and when one man could fight in both during the span of his adult life. What had happened to the human race between the years 1914 and 1945?

On September 30, 1944, the 72nd Squadron moved on to Epinal. The weather had turned bad as we left Vesoul. For the first several days after we arrived at our new assignment, it rained, fog rolled in, and the clouds hung low in the sky. But in spite of the weather, we flew almost every day.

We had to fly very low most of the time and follow railroads, roads, or any other ground reference points that went in our direction. Many times we had to turn back.

One late afternoon, a 72nd Squadron pilot left on a mission during bad weather. Added to this, at his destination he would have to land in a pasture. We all tried to return from our missions before night if possible; we knew he would return that same day if he could.

The sun was setting, and he had not come back. We began to worry. Some of us waited outside the Operations building for a while as it grew darker and darker. Finally, we decided he had stayed at his destination. A few of the pilots drifted off, but two or three of us waited a little longer.

The sky was pitch black under a high overcast when we heard the sound of the L-5 engine above. There was no light on the airfield — we observed a blackout at all times. Someone jumped in a jeep parked next to the Operations building, turned on the lights, and headed toward the upwind end of the runway. Then he stopped the vehicle and shined the lights along the runway.

We heard the engine getting closer. The throttle cut back, and out of the darkness at the end of the runway opposite the jeep came the L-5.

The pilot made a perfect landing, taxied toward the headlights of the jeep, and cut his engine. He climbed out of the plane and, standing in the glare of the headlights, took off his cap and waved it in the air.

"Whoopee!" he yelled, and fell flat on his face. The man was skunk drunk.

We piled him on the jeep. One of the other pilots taxied his L-5 to the flight line. It seems that the fellows where he had landed had a good supply of liquor, and had thrown a party — the reason why he was late.

On our second day at Epinal, we became acquainted with the Germans' love of method and regularity. But first, let me set the scene. In the Operations room there was a small wooden table that was used as a desk. Several nails had been driven into the table, and some of us had hung our mess kits on them.

Some of us pilots were standing around when we heard the sounds of an incoming engine and the chattering of a machine gun. We knew instantly we were being strafed, and we all dove for the protection of the small table at the same time. The tin mess kits banged and rattled. All of us crammed into each other in our efforts to protect ourselves under that dinky little table. The noise of our efforts, coupled with the rattle of the mess kits, created a din that almost drowned out the sound of the strafing airplane. What we had done was so stupid we all had a good laugh.

Each day at almost the same time the Germans strafed us, as if it were a milk run. But we kept our L-5s dispersed around the airfield, and damage occurred only once. However, one morning a 72nd Squadron pilot was sitting in his aircraft doing some paperwork. The pilot heard the German coming in strafing. He jumped out of his plane and fell flat onto the ground. The German hit the pilot's aircraft and punched some bullet holes in the fabric, but did little other damage. The pilot was not touched.

On October 8, 1944, one week after I had arrived at Epinal, five of us pilots were sent on Detached Service to the VI Corps in the little village of Arches, a few miles southeast of Epinal. We were closer to the front, and the pace of activity picked up considerably.

The dirt airstrip was located on top of a small hill. Our Operations section was located in a tent beside the strip. We pilots took over a large room on the second floor of a bar in Arches, set up our cots, and were quite comfortable. Posted on the walls of the bar downstairs were signs in French that warned all prostitutes that they would be arrested if they were caught plying their trade on the premises.

We began to hear the bombardment from the front lines. At night, when we were lying in our cots, the sound seemed to come through the walls of the building

A Graves Registration Detachment had begun constructing an American military cemetery near the airstrip. The entire site was surrounded by a canvas wall. Although privacy was assured from ground level, we flew right over it after takeoff and observed German POWs at work. We could see the mattress covers that held dead soldiers lying in rows alongside the newly dug graves. The POWs kept ahead in their digging. It was a solemn thought to realize those empty graves would soon hold the bodies of American soldiers who were still alive at that time.

Late one afternoon I was standing beside our Operations tent looking into the darkening afternoon eastern sky. I saw a little drama unfold, and I have often wondered who the pilots were that passed my way at that moment — for it was *only* a moment, and then it was all over.

Flying from south to north, over the battle line, was a German Messerschmitt Me-109 fighter at about 1,000 feet. Following and closing fast was an American P-51 Mustang. As they flew straight north, it became obvious the American fighter was gaining on the Me-109. Suddenly its pilot turned east and began a steep dive toward Germany. The American dove after the German and they both disappeared into the dusk of nightfall.

One cannot help but wonder what happened to the two young pilots as night fell over the battlefield. Looking back, I confess I hope both survived the war and lived the rest of their lives in peace.

Although our duties always included flying personnel and dispatches from place to place, at Arches we were close to the front. Thus, we also flew reconnaissance missions, carrying observers from our own squadron and, at times, observers from U.S. Army headquarters.

On October 13, 1944, I carried an observer on a mission to see if the Germans were still in the town of St. Die. When on reconnaissance missions, we always followed a particular flying pattern. We flew at about 2,500 feet above the ground, zigzagging continuously, and changing altitude frequently. The reason for this flight pattern was that German antiaircraft ammunition had been designed to explode above 2,500 feet and the small-arms fire from the ground could not reach us. Theoretically, if we followed that pattern we would be safe. However, someone had failed to explain this to the Germans.

I took off with my observer about the middle of the afternoon. The weather was good, and we had fine visibility. As we approached St. Die, the observer unleashed his binoculars and began to sweep the area. For some reason the front was relatively quiet. I wandered over the town. My observer remained silent, looking about with his binoculars.

Then an explosion occurred right behind me! My first thought was that my observer had fired his .45-caliber pistol behind my head. I looked back. To my rear was a big, black cloud — the smoke of an exploded .88-caliber German shell. I knew the next one would be closer, or maybe right on target. I rolled the aircraft upside down and went into a straight dive. The next explosion was right where I had been. I kept diving until I was close to the ground. When I leveled out, I sped toward home.

We had learned what we needed to — the Germans were still in St. Die.

Late one afternoon a group of us were standing outside our Operations tent next to the landing strip. One of the pilots looked up and yelled, "Look out!" as he pointed toward the east.

We all followed his direction. Coming in right on top of us was a P-47 Thunderbolt, one of America's most powerful and effective fighter aircraft. We heard no sound from its engine, as it glided in. A gliding P-47 drops like a brick. The plane came down over our heads and headed silently into the woods. The sound of its impact was that of a 1,000 tin cans hitting a lumber yard. The aircraft went in with such force that it cut a swath through the grove of trees.

We all ran to the scene, and when we arrived, the pilot was climbing out of the cockpit. He did not have a scratch on him. He looked to be about 20 years old, and a young 20 at that. He was pink-cheeked, as if he had never shaved in his life. He had a broad smile on his face, but no sign of fear or shock. He had come within an inch of losing his life, and he was acting as if it were an everyday occurrence. He explained that his engine had taken a hit, which had blown out a piston.

He called his squadron from our Operations tent, and shortly a jeep arrived to take him back to his base. I am sure that in a few days he had a new P-47 to fly and was back in the war.

On October 21, 1944, I was called upon to carry another distinguished passenger — William Randolph Hearst, Jr., the son of the legendary publisher. I carried Hearst from Arches to Nancy, France. Little did I know then that his daughter Patty Hearst, years later, would achieve notoriety when she was kidnapped and participated with her kidnappers in a bank robbery.

Hearst, Jr., was an accredited war correspondent. War correspondents wore military uniforms with no rank showing, except a circular identification patch sewed to the left shoulder of their uniform. They were allowed to go almost anywhere. It was not unusual for one of our pilots to carry a war correspondent over the front lines and, in some instances, beyond.

One afternoon just before we were to go to our billet in the big room over the bar, the officer in charge of our detachment called us all into the Operations tent and gave us a little speech. In effect, he told us that an American battalion had been cut off in a box canyon east of Bruyères. They had attacked up the canyon, and the Germans came in behind them. The Germans occupied the hills around the canyon, and were firing down on the battalion. The Americans needed medical supplies and ammunition.

"As you can see," he said, "we have a low overcast, and supply planes can't go into those hills to drop supplies."

The officer pulled out a map of the region and we all gathered around him. He placed a finger on a spot on the map.

"The battalion is here," he noted. "Right now this overcast is lying practically on the tops of the surrounding mountains. You can get in there and drop the supplies by flying at about two hundred feet."

We all knew what was coming next, and we didn't like it a bit.

"You've got to watch out for German small-arms fire going in, for the Germans are firing from the hillside. After you drop the supplies, you've got to turn around at the end of the canyon and do it all over again on the way back."

We did not like any of this at all.

"This is strictly a voluntary mission," the officer continued. "In the morning, at first light, if you volunteer, show up here at the Operations tent. We'll load your plane, and you can take off. If you don't volunteer, then you can continue flying as usual and nothing will ever be said, nor will anything go on your military record."

With that, he dismissed us. We went to our big room over the bar. The matter was not mentioned as we gathered in our billet. This was one of those suicide missions you often heard about, and the reality of the situation took all the romance right out of it. I imagine my feelings were much the same as the other pilots. I did not want to fly it. The way the mission had been presented to us, there was no way we could pull it off. Flying under a low ceiling at about 200 feet above the ground with Germans firing from high ground on both sides, then turning around in a narrow valley and flying back the same way, running the gauntlet again, had disaster written all over it.

We moped around our room for a while doing little useless chores. Then one of the fellows began to write his last will and testament. He mentioned what he was doing out loud and a couple of other fellows did the same. Several of the pilots wrote letters.

I sat on my cot and worried. I had already written my last will and testament. There was no other choice. I was sure of one thing, though. I was not going to be the first to back out of the deal and be disgraced for life. And the fact that no one backed out was, I believe, the key to all of us volunteering. It was an all-or-nothing deal.

And thus, I learned what makes soldiers volunteer for suicide missions. It's not heroism, it's pride.

The next morning, every pilot turned up ready to go, only to discover that the mission had been scrubbed. The battalion had been rescued by a regiment that broke through the German line during the night.

There is no doubt in my mind that every pilot would have gone in with supplies and medicine. But they wouldn't have liked it.

Chapter 10

O N NOVEMBER 4, 1944, our detachment moved up to Grandvilliers instead of returning to our squadron at Epinal. Our arrival was not without incident. Whoever had chosen the landing site had made a serious mistake. The field was a sloping pasture bordered by trees. If that was not bad enough, the rain-soaked ground was soft — almost too soft.

I could tell on my approach the field was too short and the trees were too close. I set full flaps and throttled back almost to a stall. When I touched down, I felt the ground give. I began braking as soon as I felt safe and came to a stop just short of the trees. I taxied off to one side, climbed out of my L-5, and stood watching as my compadres took a try. Only one aircraft hit a tree and sheered off a wing. But the field was totally unacceptable for operations.

The weather became so bad with rain and low ceilings that we could not fly anyway. In the meantime, while we left our aircraft in the field where we had landed them, the Army Engineers prepared a runway a short distance away. However, this strip had its own disadvantages. The Engineers had laid out interlocking steel sections called PSP — perforated steel plate — in a straight line, which gave us plenty of length in which to land. But the strip was only about 20 feet wide. Furthermore, the Engineers ran the strip parallel to a line of trees, which formed a barrier about 20 feet off to one side, for the length of the runway.

Two real problems were built into this layout. First, the strip looked like a narrow ribbon upon approach, and the trees appeared to be a solid wall as the pilot flew down the strip. Any side wind could cause the aircraft to drift only a few feet before the wing hit the trees. Second, when the steel was wet, it was slick as ice.

As soon as the rains stopped, however, we moved our L-5s over to our new steel runway. We learned soon enough just how rough flying was going to get. My first landing was an adventure. I came in on my approach with full flaps down, crabbing into the wind. Just before hitting the steel strip, I straightened up and dropped my right wheel. I held the aircraft straight on the wheel as I stalled out and dropped the left wheel onto the strip. I could feel the wheels trying to slide, but they didn't. I had plenty of length and guided the aircraft as evenly down that strip as I could.

Every pilot landed successfully, and every pilot felt just like I did. We were basically very glad we had the steel strip, even with some handicaps. It, nevertheless, was going to be a confidence builder.

During our entire stay at Grandvilliers the weather was so bad we hardly flew at all. It was rainy, cloudy, foggy, and turning colder. Time did not hang heavy, however. We had good tents with wooden floors, gasoline heaters, and generators that provided us with electricity. The engineers had placed our tents close to a forest.

A few of us took a day off and went into Plombières, in a narrow valley reached by a winding road down the side of a mountain. Plombières looked like a calendar picture of an Alpine village. We were in the Vosges Mountains, a region well known for its hot springs. So while we were in the town, we went to a bath house. The big tub was as large as four ordinary bathtubs, and the water was so hot it had to be cooled. I lay in the warm water for an hour, just soaking. It was wonderful for I had not had a bath in weeks.

On another day a couple of us fellows took a walk down a dirt road. We noticed some soldiers coming in our direction, but we did not pay much attention to them until several of them yelled at us to back off. We backed up slowly, almost stepping in our tracks. When the soldiers got near us, we saw they were "sappers" — they were sweeping for land mines. We had almost stumbled into a mine field.

During this period when we were flying very few missions, we had an opportunity to catch up on our L-5's maintenance. All scheduled inspections and maintenance were performed back at Epinal. If the problem was minor, we waited and flew back to Grandvilliers the same day. If more work was required, we could catch a ride back to our detachment. Then in a day or so, Master Sergeant Tom Vernelli would deliver the aircraft to our encampment.

Although Tom was a rated liaison pilot, he did not fly any missions. As line chief, he was responsible for all aircraft maintenance. He was very good at the job and saw to it that our L-5s were properly inspected and repaired after damage.

I do not recall just when Tom came into the 72nd Squadron, but it had to be before we had been shipped overseas. I became aware of him when we had received our aircraft in Italy; he had supervised their assembly. At first I wondered who that old man was, wearing the liaison wings. We considered anyone above 30 years of age to be an "old man." However, I could tell he knew aircraft and he could supervise men. We all liked him. No one resented that he did not fly missions. He had a humorous disposition and got along well with all of us, though I do not recall anyone mixing socially with him. While the rest of us were gaining experience in flying under all conditions, Tom was working on our aircraft.

One rainy and blustery day, Tom delivered an aircraft to our field. I watched him as he approached the narrow, steel strip. I knew by the way the aircraft was drifting that he was in trouble. When he came below the level of the tops of the trees, he drifted into them. The impact sheered off the wing back to the strut. Tom gave the aircraft full throttle and veered off to the right. The plane kept flying with about four feet of its left wing gone. We watched his aircraft wobble back toward Epinal. Surprisingly he made it.

But Tom's inexperience finally did him in. The weather stayed bad and the clouds hung low. There were overcast days when we did fly, but we learned soon enough, in that unfamiliar country, to fly high enough to clear any lines. If we could not fly that high, we did not fly.

Apparently Tom did not take that into consideration when he started to deliver an aircraft one day. He flew into a high line and was killed instantly. He was buried near Epinal. Tom was a very good man, and we all missed him.

Sergeant Kurt Wottke took over Tom's duties. He was well qualified and did an excellent job of supervising the maintenance of our aircraft for the duration of the war.

We left Grandvilliers on November 30, 1944, and returned to our squadron in Epinal. I flew a mission from Epinal to Sarrebourg and was ordered to continue on to Strasbourg, where I would join a recently arrived detachment. The flight to Sarrebourg was not easy. Although the weather had improved a bit, the clouds were still low, and fog hung on the ground in places. I followed some roads through the Vosges valleys and made the flight without incident. But I did not go as the crow flies. The nearly two-hour trip had been very tiring.

The next morning, flying from Sarrebourg to Strasbourg was somewhat easier because I skirted the foothills of the Vosges Mountains. When I reached the Saverne Gap, I came out onto the broad, flat Rhine River plain. After the flight through the mountains, the plain was quite pleasant. The small Alsatian villages were undamaged. I saw a couple of stork nests on chimney tops. A slight fog hung over the valley, but was burning off as I approached the airfield west of Strasbourg. All in all it had been a pleasant flight.

The airfield had been a major German installation that included a number of brick barracks and a large Operations building with a control tower. Surprisingly, the long concrete runways were hardly damaged.

Except for a couple of L-5s sitting near the Operations building, the place was deserted. I soon found out that the interior of some of the buildings had been trashed. I don't know if the damage had been done by departing Germans or scrounging GIs.

Five of us made up the detachment at Strasbourg. We moved into one of the German barracks that had hardly been touched, and we lived like kings. Three of us fixed up a room with lockers, tables, and a stove. At night we had lights provided by a German diesel generator. But at all times we observed strict blackout procedures by covering the windows. And there were showers. All we had to do was fire up the boilers.

We stayed in Strasbourg only a week, and I flew just three missions. However, during our short stay, we had nightly visitors. Just as we were about to turn in on the first night, we heard the familiar sound of a German bomber. We made a run for a half-full potato cellar that we had discovered under the barracks. The German aircraft came in low and dropped its bomb near another barracks. He missed us. After waiting a while in the cellar we returned to find Master Sergeant Lester Sloan sleeping like a baby on his cot.

Every night the German plane flew over and dropped a bomb. Every night all of us, except Sloan, ran to the potato cellar. Every night he got a good night's rest, and we lost a lot of sleep. After a few of days of this I felt a little foolish and decided I would not go to the cellar. About the time the bomber usually came over, Sloan began to undress for bed. I did too. The rest of the pilots stayed dressed. With the first sound of the German's engine, the other pilots headed down the stairs. I crawled onto my cot and covered up my head. As the sound of the bomber came closer, I began to ponder the situation: I was the guy that crawled under the jeep; I was the guy that dug a foxhole. I realized I was crazy to stay there, for one of those nights that German was going to hit his target.

Before the German could drop his bomb, I jumped off my cot and ran for the cellar. He again missed our barracks by 100 yards. But I did not feel foolish at all!

The war was static on this front. The Americans had not yet crossed the Rhine River, which ran through the heart of Strasbourg. The Germans held the east side and the Americans held the west side. All the major fighting was going on to the north of us. The only action occurred when the adversaries took pot shots at each other across the river.

Interestingly, the buildings along the river were apartment houses. Therefore, the opposing sides were actually occupying comfortable quarters while firing occasionally at each other. Neither side had orders to attack or retreat at this time. They just fired their guns to make the other side keep their heads down.

After our short stay in Strasbourg we moved on to Steinbourg, a small village a few miles northeast of Saverne. No high lines or trees were near the flat, dirt landing strip. It was excellent for our purposes.

We took over a small building located on the road that ran past the west boundary of the field. There was a room for our cots, a room we could use for dining, and even a kitchen — quite adequate for our purposes. We received a good supply of food, which we stored in the kitchen.

A day or so after we had arrived, a lady and her daughter came to us and wanted to cook and clean for us. We knew the woman only as Mamma. Her daughter, Denise, was about 15 years old. We paid them with food. At the end of the day, just before they went home, we gave them an armload of canned goods. It was a very good arrangement for both parties.

We were much busier at Steinbourg than we had been at Strasbourg. The weather cleared somewhat and we flew almost every day. We were much closer to the front lines and could hear the bombardment quite clearly at night. Flying out of Steinbourg became grim. One mission carried me near Haguenau. The day before my flight there had been a fire fight for the Haguenau airport, just south of town. As I flew over, I could see dead bodies scattered near the end of the runway. I concluded they were German bodies, for our Graves Registration Detachment usually removed American casualties very soon after a battle.

On another flight to St. Die, I landed near a small village called Saales. The place was so fresh from battle that there were many signs with "BODY" painted on them, pointing toward a cluster of weeds or a ditch. In a building occupied by a small group of soldiers, I found a German helmet with a bullet hole. I figured it would make a good souvenir. But kicking it over, I saw part of the German's head. I left it where I had found it.

About this time, my leather flying jacket had a damaged zipper. I couldn't zip it up, so I removed the zipper and held my jacket together with my gun belt. This was a very unsatisfactory solution. One day I found a coat with a zipper. I carefully removed it and planned, at my first chance, to have it installed on my leather jacket.

I found an old tailor in Steinbourg. He could not speak a word of English, and I could not speak a word of German or French, whichever language he spoke. But we managed to communicate enough for him to understand what I wanted. I left my jacket and the zipper with him. In a few days I returned to pick it up. He had finished the job, and I tried the jacket on. But the zipper had been too long, and when he had cut it to the right length, he had cut off the fastener. He had tucked the ruined ends very neatly under the seam of the jacket. It was one of the neatest jobs of destruction I have ever seen.

I could not chew him out, because we did not speak each other's language. As I left, he laughed and chortled happily. Surely the old rascal knew what a zipper was and how to install it properly. Was it sabotage? Who knows? I wore the jacket unzipped through the rest of the war.

Chapter 11

AS THE MONTH of December wore on, the weather turned colder. Some days were cloudy with sprinkles of snow. Winter was moving in fast.

The frozen Marne-Rhine Canal ran close by Steinbourg. I found a pair of ice skates in the house where we were staying, strapped them on, and tried my hand at skating. I was a much better pilot than ice skater.

One of those rare moments happened when we first had arrived at Steinbourg, a moment of no real significance but one I will never forget.

One freezing cold night, when the sky was clear and a full moon hung over the eastern horizon, I stepped outside the house. The night was calm; even the guns at the front were quiet. I walked a short way and stood in the silence. From somewhere in the distance, I could not tell from what direction, I heard someone playing a harmonica. The sound was perfectly clear, and I could hear every note. The song was "Lili Marlene," which the American Army troops had adopted from the *Afrika Korps* in North Africa. I stood very quietly and listened until the music ended. Then I went back inside the house.

I did not mention the moment to my comrades. I have never felt so lonesome before or after that moment in eastern France.

On December 16, 1944, the Germans launched a counteroffensive against the Allied front in the Ardennes Forest. This attack would soon be known as the Battle of the Bulge, because a "bulge" in the line began to appear on the Allies' situation maps.

At first we were not overly concerned. The action was north of us in another sector, and we did not have a personal interest in it. We had our own problems. In addition, the news we received was largely by word of mouth. We had no regular newspapers and rarely listened to the news on the radio. However, several days later we realized something serious was taking place north of us.

The eight of us in our detachment were flying every day. Christmas was approaching, and we had begun planning well in advance. We gathered all the wine, schnapps, beer, and champagne we could find. Our Lieutenant spent considerable time making place cards and menus, and we borrowed plates and glasses.

Our celebration started Christmas Eve night. We opened the liquid refreshments and got really drunk. Christmas morning I had a royal hangover. I was physically sick and so jumpy I could not stand any noise. I took pills of some sort and finally, about noon, felt better, but I was still shaky. Then I had to fly a Captain to Montbéliard, a trip of about an hour and half each way. Imagine that, a three-hour mission on Christmas Day, and me with a hangover that would stagger a giant.

Sunset came early in the winter. If I did not get back by 5 p.m., it would be too dark to fly. I had to leave Montbéliard no later than 3 p.m. on the dot, or I could not get back for our Christmas party. The flight went without incident, but I told the Captain if he did not return to the plane by 3:30, I was leaving without him. He did not show up, so I left — I had a Christmas party waiting for me. I landed after dark. The other fellows had been sweating whether I would arrive in time. The table was already set, and the Christmas candle had been lit. Everyone was cleaned up and in uniform.

I hurriedly washed up and put on a jacket. We all sat down. What a banquet! Four candles stuck in beer bottles sat on each corner of the table, with a small Christmas tree in the middle. It had been decorated with chaff — tin foil dropped by German aircraft to fool our radar.

The turkey was perfectly cooked and made us feel like royalty. I ate turkey and dressing until I had to loosen my belt. Then came dessert. The people of Steinbourg had given us some pies and cakes. Each of us had a plate piled high with pastry.

I had been drinking champagne with my meal, but I took coffee with my dessert. Finally, when we finished eating, we all sat back to relax and smoke. I felt the Christmas spirit, and for a short time I was happy.

Then, our nightly caller flew over, followed by a big explosion. We grabbed our helmets and ran outside. We were just in time to see the German aircraft flying away, his guns wide open. About 100 yards across the landing strip we could see a large, bright light. He had dropped a stick of incendiaries and fragmentation bombs. However, he had missed our aircraft; his bombs had landed on bare ground.

We had been keeping a close watch on the Battle of the Bulge. We were concerned, but we were also watching the Germans right in front of us. Then, a part of the German line wheeled south, extending the bulge toward our location.

The first news we heard that a move was imminent was early that evening. Our CO called us from Sarrebourg and told us to return to our squadron first thing the next morning. Some of my laundry was at an older woman's house in Steinbourg, and I immediately went into town to get it. I was gone for a long time because she was not home. I had spent valuable time trying to locate her, but failed to do so. I returned to the field to find

ROAST TURKEY
SAGE DRESSING
MASHED POTATOES GRAVEY
CREAMED PEAS

PLAIN CAKE   FRUIT CAKE
CUSTARD PIE   MINCE PIE

ROUGE WINE   CHAMPAGNE
        CANDY   NUTS
        COFFEE

CHRISTMAS

MENU
1944

T/SGT BRYCE   72ND LIAISON SQ DETACHMENT

Our "official" Christmas 1944 menu.

considerable excitement. As I walked in the door, the Lieutenant was packing.

"How much night flying have you had?" he asked excitedly.

"Enough," I said, for I could see we were on the move. I could wait for details later.

I went through to my room where bedlam reigned. The pilots were packing quickly, and as I started gathering my things they gave me the details.

Our CO had called while I was gone. "Burn everything," he said, "and meet the squadron where we stayed longest."

"But what about the aircraft?" our Lieutenant had asked.

"My God!" the CO exclaimed. "Pack everything and send it by vehicle. If you hear small-arms fire, fly the aircraft out. If the weather is bad, burn the planes, and get out the best way you can!"

We had stayed the longest in Epinal on the Moselle River, about 50 miles west of Steinbourg — obviously the place he meant. The reason for moving out had to be either a German breakthrough or an American withdrawal. From the heavy sound of the artillery, we determined it had to be a breakthrough. We still remembered how the Germans had broken through at St. Vith, and we were afraid they had done the same on this front.

We had plenty of food stored, and it soon became obvious we could not take it along. We decided to give all the goods to Mamma and Denise. They had been good workers and we had become attached to them. It was a lot of food for one family, and despite the excitement, Mamma supervised its loading in a calm and business-like manner. Let the Germans break through, let the war go on for an eternity . . . it didn't matter to Mamma now. We piled the weapons carrier high and took Mamma and Denise with their food into town.

We arrived at Mamma's house and began unloading, when the uproar began. Mamma's husband started yelling at us, grabbing the food, and carrying it back to the weapons carrier. We finally figured out what was wrong. He did not want the returning Germans to find all that American food in his house. Mamma and her husband yelled it out in the front yard, but Mamma won. But he would not touch a can, so the driver and I helped Mamma and Denise carry it all inside. Mamma's husband had disappeared into the back.

Crying, Mamma and Denise both gave the driver and me a great big hug and kiss and wished us a safe journey.

We drove back to the field, finished loading the vehicles, and sent our Operations clerk and two mechanics on their way to Epinal. They were very frightened and were ready to leave.

By that time, the artillery seemed much louder. Blacked-out convoys began passing by on the road, all moving to the rear. We warmed our L-5s, glanced at the weather (it was a beautiful night), and began our vigil in the Operations room.

We thought we had given Mamma all of our food, but we found some steaks, coffee, eggs, and bread that we had missed. We decided we could not leave all that food for the Germans to find, so we began cooking up a meal. Outside we could hear the soft purr of passing convoys and an occasional shifting gear. In the distance, the heavy, steady rumble of the enemy artillery seemed to be getting closer. We kept an anxious eye on the telephone, waiting for our CO to tell us to fly out.

We ate a big meal. We couldn't possibly eat all the steaks, but we ate quite a few, while the war went on around us. Two officers who had become lost from their convoy came in, and we fed them until they could not eat any more. Then a U.S. Army signalman arrived and tried to take away our telephone, but we would not allow it. Our Lieutenant signed for it. We gave the soldier a cup of coffee and sent him on his way. Ten minutes later, we found the telephone dead anyway.

By then we knew we would have to wait to leave until the Germans were practically on top of us. We decided to post a guard and go to bed. I took a long drink of schnapps and opened my bedroll, lay down, and tried to sleep. On the floor, with my ear so close to the ground, I could hear the artillery so loud it seemed right over the hill. Perhaps the schnapps helped me to get a little sleep. I managed a short snooze in each two-hour period between getting up and warming my aircraft. But all hell was breaking loose someplace close by, and it was hard to get any sleep at all.

We flew out the next morning, just as dawn was breaking in the east. We could barely see the boundaries of the landing strip. Half an hour later, I landed in Epinal. Major Percy, our CO, met each aircraft as we pulled up to the flight line and shook our hands.

I felt like I was at a class reunion. Pilots and mechanics from all the detachments near the front had returned, and we all had stories to tell.

For the first time in weeks, the 72nd Liaison Squadron was assembled again.

But we did not stay long in Epinal. The next morning we flew to Luneville, where we were going to stay through the worst of the winter of 1944-1945.

Chapter 12

WE HAD A unique landing arrangement at Luneville. It was not safe, but we managed the best we could. Just east of town, our strip ran north and south. It was a good solid strip, and plenty long enough for us to land. However, just east of us, the P-47 landing strip ran east and west. When the Thunderbolts took off on a mission, they passed right over our runway. When we took off or landed, we really had to keep our heads up. Surprisingly, none of us ever had a close call with the fighters.

I did have one close call, but it was not with a P-47. One afternoon shortly after we had arrived at Luneville, I drew a mission back to Epinal. The weather was bad, and I did not want to get caught there. It was late when I started back. Fog was collecting in places, and the clouds were close to the ground. I flew at about 200 feet, following the Moselle River and the railroad north to where it left the river and went to Luneville. Rain began, and I knew the P-47s would not be flying.

The arrow points to our billet in the City Hall of a small town east of Luneville. We slept on the second floor. Two windows to the right of the door opened to our dining room.

I was about 100 feet above the ground on my landing approach and could hardly see anything. Suddenly, out of the clouds and rain on my left, a British Spitfire streaked across my path to land on the P-47 strip. I don't believe he was more than 300 feet in front of me when he passed — a very close call indeed.

Several of us pilots and a mechanic or two took over the City Hall in a small village east of Luneville, for our billet. We hired a young lady and her brother to cook and clean for us. We set up our cots and settled in for the winter.

The winter weather came in waves, each a little worse than the last. When it was cold, there would be a high cloud overcast. We could fly on those days. Then it snowed, covering the ground, and flying was more difficult. Some days when it snowed, the overcast was low; flying was touch-and-go. Then, the snows came in earnest, covering the landing strip. We couldn't fly.

Some days, dawn broke on a snow-frozen earth. The sky was clear and the cold intense. On one of those cold, clear days, we stood witness to one of those phenomenons of World War II. About the middle of the morning we could hear a deep roar from the sky to the northwest. Hundreds of B-17 Flying Fortresses, flying in V formations, were coming our way at about 20,000 feet. Above the B-17s, gleaming, silver P-51 Mustang escorts zigzagged back and forth, to intercept German fighter attacks. Approaching Luneville, the aircraft flew into a large wheeling maneuver.

Shortly a flight of B-24 Liberators appeared from the southeast, joining the great circle. By the time both groups had completed one circle, they had merged into a large formation and were headed directly east toward Germany.

We pilots stood in awe at the panorama in the clear sky above us. Many thoughts crossed our minds about the significance of what we were witnessing. I think, though, that one of us summed it up as we watched the immense formation pass overhead.

"There are lots of Germans alive right now that won't be alive when the sun sets," he said.

What we thought, but left unspoken, was that the same could be said

Dining in our billet in a small town outside Luneville. On the far side of the table (from r to l) is Master Sergeant Lester R. Sloan, Technical Sergeant Eugene W. Woods, Staff Sergeant Vernon R. Parish, (unknown officer), and Technical Sergeant James R. Bryce.

about the American flight crews and fighter pilots in those immense formations.

One afternoon someone yelled, "Look there!" and pointed toward the east. Coming in low, a bomber with one or more engines inoperable was trying to make it to the P-47 strip. A red flare shot out one of the gun ports. The ambulances headed for the runway. By the time the bomber had come to a stop, the ambulances were alongside. The medics and able-bodied crew members began unloading the wounded and dead fliers.

As the weather turned colder, we finally had to have some place at the landing strip where we could stay warm while waiting for our mission assignments. The engineers had set up a tent with a wooden floor and walls, which protected us from the rain. However, in extremely cold weather, we may as well have been in a freezer.

When we learned of a welder at headquarters who could build us a stove for the tent, one of the pilots took our design and arranged to have it built. A few days later, we were notified to come and get our heater. With joy in our hearts we soon had it installed. The upright stove consisted of a section of 12-inch pipe sealed at both ends. An opening at the bottom, about six inches wide and three inches high, provided a space to light the fire.

At the top, a line with a valve led outside the tent to a can of gasoline placed high enough so that it would gravity-feed into the stove. The theory was that we could adjust the valve to allow just a drop or two of fuel to drip to the bottom of the stove, burn, and provide heat.

We all crowded around for the first lighting of the stove. One of the fellows very carefully adjusted the valve, starting the slow drip. He lit a match and stuck it into the opening. The fire started and we all stood back, listening to the warming sounds of our own heater. Then, the loudest boom I ever heard roared out of the stove, and the tent flopped out like a balloon. We scattered for the entrance like a bunch of scared bulls, each of us trying to be the first outside.

We had not designed a heating stove, we had designed a gasoline-

Snowed in at Luneville. Technical Sergeant James R. Bryce standing (third from r) in front of a Stinson L-5.

powered bomb! We stood around outside in the cold trying to figure out what had happened and what to do next. One of our braver souls finally looked inside the tent. The explosion had blown out the fire, but the gasoline was still dripping into the heater. Someone went inside and turned the valve off, then scurried back outside.

We tried, on one or two occasions, to adjust the valve so that the heater would work, but it blew up every time. The tent remained cold.

We did get one good laugh out of the fiasco. One cold and bitter day we were standing near the runway when a couple of pilots flew in from another squadron. They claimed to be freezing, and we told them there was a heater in the tent. We instructed them to turn the valve just a little bit, and light the gasoline dripping on the bottom of the heater.

They disappeared into the tent and we waited. In about five minutes we heard the explosion. The snow on the top of the tent rose about a foot and fell back onto the canvas, sliding off onto the ground. The pilots ran out of the tent like scared rabbits. They were so frightened they forgot to be mad at us.

One night I was asleep when suddenly a high, piercing, screaming sound woke me. I thought it was coming right in on top of me. Then there was a loud explosion not far away. I thought it might have been a bomb, but I could do nothing about it, so I went back to sleep.

The next morning I found out it had not been a bomb at all, but a British bomber that had been hit in a night raid and had crashed on the way home. I went to the crash site, but I could not see an aircraft, only a deep, elongated, smoking indention. The bomber had either disintegrated or burrowed itself into the ground. I heard later that the crew had bailed out. I hoped so.

At about this time, one morning, I was assigned to fly an officer to Metz, the site of General George S. Patton's headquarters, then return him to Luneville — a flight of about an hour. I landed on a small strip south of the town. Apparently it had been a private field, for it was not well cared for. The only building was a tin hangar to the north. A couple of L-5s were sitting on the east edge of the field, near the end of the landing strip.

I taxied to the hangar and let my passenger out. A driver was waiting for him in a jeep, and they drove off toward Metz. I had an hour to kill, so I strolled out to the other L-5s, looked them over, then strolled back toward my aircraft.

Suddenly a jeep sped toward me, skidding to a stop right in front of me. An MP jumped out.

"My God!" he yelled, right in my face. "Get out of sight!"

I was so startled, I didn't know what to do. Were we being strafed or bombed? He shoved me toward the side of the hangar, pushing me completely out of sight of the other L-5s.

"General Patton's coming!" he explained. "Stay out of sight!"

"*What?*"

"You're out of uniform, for God's sake!" he yelled. "Stay out of sight until he's gone!"

I was out of uniform, all right. I was wearing paratrooper's boots, winter brown trousers, a summer tan shirt, no tie, a leather jacket with a broken zipper, and a billed cap. But who cared? We were at war, weren't we?

Well, General George S. Patton, Jr., cared.

Several jeeps rounded a curve in the road followed by the General's. Each jeep was equipped with a swivel-mounted machine gun manned by a very well-dressed gunner. Patton was standing at parade attention on a specially modified rear seat, holding onto a circular bar. I noticed that his uniform was as far out of regulation as mine. He was wearing a chrome-plated steel helmet, Eisenhower jacket, cavalry jodhpurs, and leather riding boots. Strapped to his waist was a chrome-plated .45-caliber six-shooter.

The only difference between General George S. Patton's non-regulation uniform and Technical Sergeant James R. Bryce's uniform was that his was clean and mine was dirty. Patton and his entourage looked like they had all just stepped out of a shower into new uniforms. My uniform had not been washed in weeks, and I had not had a bath or a haircut in a long, long time.

Patton's jeep carried him to one of the L-5s parked near the end of the runway. He crawled into the back seat of the aircraft. His pilot, a Captain, by the way, climbed into the front seat, and they took off. His entourage went back up the road and disappeared around the curve.

The more I look back on that event, in view of Patton's well-documented penchant for creating examples for enlisted soldiers, the more I believe I could have been in serious trouble if I had not been warned and hidden by that MP riding picket on Patton's convoy.

The only good thing I care to say about General Patton is that he was an excellent General. His forces had played an integral role in the Battle of the Bulge.

During World War II, we were blessed with great Commanders — Generals Alexander M. Patch, Dwight D. Eisenhower, Jacob L. Devers, Omar Bradley, Lucien K. Truscott, Douglas MacArthur, James "Jimmy" Doolittle, to name a few. Not only were they great military tacticians, but they were great role models for the troops as well. These Generals were soldiers who wore the proper military uniform with pride. But Patton was a peacock, and a potentially dangerous peacock at that. Witness his action that had cost him his last command, in Sicily. Patton had been reported for striking a shell-shocked soldier in a hospital.

On March 16, 1945, I was on the flight line waiting for a mission when our Operations officer approached and handed me a manila envelope, filled with "news dispatches," he said. I was to take them to Paris and give them to a Sergeant there, at the *Café de la Paix*. If he was not at the *Café*, I was to go to the Hotel Scribe.

The Sergeant could be considered our unofficial press agent. It was rumored that his father was the editor of a major newspaper, and therefore the Sergeant had been assigned to fly most of the news men who showed up at our headquarters. This also allowed the Sergeant time to see Paris occasionally.

"Where will I land?" I asked.

"At Orly. You'll see it when you get close to Paris."

That was all the instructions I had. I folded my map so I could follow a route from Luneville to Paris, and took off.

The weather was not good. The overcast was high, but fog banks lay about the countryside. About halfway to Paris, I ran into fog and low-lying clouds and looked for a place to land. I found a smooth meadow on which to put down and pulled over to a fence that ran alongside a road. I climbed out of my aircraft and strolled over to the fence to smoke a cigarette and wait for better weather.

I began to pay attention to something that would become more and more pronounced the farther our Allied Armies advanced. Many people were walking in both directions along the road. As war action nears or passes by, the civilians try to get out of the way. Their lives have been disrupted, and they have to seek safety. And so they move away from danger. When the threat is gone, they return home; but they have to walk. As we moved farther toward Germany, and especially within Germany, the roads were crowded with civilians, mostly women, children, and the elderly, walking in both directions.

A very attractive girl left the road and approached me. She was French, but she spoke good English. She asked for a cigarette, then she told me she was trying to get to her home in Paris. She had walked a long way and still had a long way to go. She explained to me how the people in the cities and villages had left their homes to escape the war as it rolled their way.

The fog soon burned off, and I gave her another cigarette. Then I took off and headed for Paris.

Orly is one of the busiest airports in the world. During World War II, its traffic was almost exclusively military. As I approached, I could see the rows of military planes lined up on the tarmac. I had no radio, so I had to circle the airport and wait for a green light. Needless to say, I kept my eyes peeled for any other aircraft in the landing pattern.

After I had set down, I pulled up to the flight line and gassed up. Then I found a place to park my L-5 and headed into Paris on a city bus. I had a strange feeling — from the front lines after flying in bad weather, staying in small villages, and seeing the horrors of war almost daily. I suddenly found myself on a city bus on a busy street, in a city full of people who looked like they did not know that a war was going on.

Late in the afternoon I arrived at the *Café de la Paix*. I still had not had a bath in weeks, and I was completely out of uniform. Except for my liaison wings pinned to my shirt, I showed no rank. I entered and sat down at a table in what many people have said is one of the most cosmopolitan restaurants in the world. If a person sits at a table on the sidewalk of the *Café de la Paix* long enough, it is said, that person will see everyone in the world walk past at least once.

As outlandish as I looked, the waiter was as polite as if I had been a

General. He could speak some English, and when I told him I was waiting for someone, he quietly left.

A very beautiful young lady was sitting alone at a table near me. When I looked at her, our eyes met and she smiled in a very friendly manner. On the second look she bowed her head slightly for me to come to her table.

I joined her. She could speak a little English. Her first words were, "Do you have a cigarette?"

I gave her one, and she lit it and took a deep drag, slowly letting the smoke drift out of her mouth.

"Could I have another one for later?" she asked.

Oh, my yes, she sure could. Her smile and attitude was glorious. I had heard good stories about French women.

"I'm a war hero," I said. A little bragging always helped.

"Oh!" she said, her eyes wide.

"I just flew in from the front lines," I continued. "The weather was real bad. I had to make a forced landing."

"How much money do you have?" she asked, which was not at all what I wanted to talk about.

I looked into my wallet. So did she. She reached out and spread it open and smiled.

"I'm sorry," she said. "I can't spend the night with you."

"I have an extra pack of cigarettes. Never been opened."

I took the unopened pack from my pocket and held it toward her.

"Thank you," she said, taking the cigarettes from me and dropping them into her purse.

From there on the conversation played out fast. I decided I had been stood up by the Sergeant, so I left the beautiful girl in the *Café* and headed for the Hotel Scribe, only a short distance away. I had no doubt where I would find the Sergeant. I went directly to the bar.

The place was off limits to enlisted men, but I didn't have any rank showing. I was under orders to deliver a packet, so I went in and looked around. I found the Sergeant right where I thought I would, standing at the bar drinking and holding forth with other war correspondents. I gave him the packet and ordered a cognac.

After an initial drink, he took my arm and ushered me across to a table surrounded by a crowd of soldiers and correspondents. He introduced me to a very important man, Ed Kennedy, head of the Associated Press

Foreign Office. I did not know how important a person Kennedy was until a few months later. He was the individual who, in violation of General Eisenhower's specific orders, had prematurely released the news of the German surrender. When the Germans had signed the documents, the reporters who had been invited to the event had absolute orders not to release the information until the Russians had been notified. Then it could be put out by all of the Allies simultaneously.

But Kennedy wanted the scoop of a lifetime, so he released the item early, and created a diplomatic incident with the Russians. General Eisenhower threw the reporter out of Europe immediately, and Kennedy's reputation was ruined.

Drinking cognac, I stood near the crowded table and listened to the correspondents argue and brag for a long time. I was fascinated by their stories of places and wars on which they had reported. I drank so much cognac that my first recollection was of a hotel employee shaking me awake the next morning. I had fallen asleep on the divan in the hallway, just outside the bar. I had a hangover only cognac in large doses can produce.

My flight back to Luneville was sheer misery. Thank goodness the weather stayed good. All I had to do was point the aircraft toward my destination and keep the windows down. I needed all the fresh air I could get.

Then on March 23, 1945, the 72nd Liaison Squadron went to Saarguemines, on the German frontier. Spring was coming, the weather was getting better, and we were moving into Germany.

Chapter 13

WE STAYED IN Sarreguemines only five days. But we had received an appropriate reception upon our arrival. As soon as I landed and pulled up beside the strip, one of the other pilots came to my L-5.

"We've got a reception committee," he said.

I climbed out of my aircraft and followed him as he led me to two dead German soldiers lying near one of our tents. The dehydrated corpses, still relatively well-preserved, had been there throughout the cold days of the winter. They each had Red Cross arm bands, and empty holsters were attached to their belts. Each corpse had a long piece of cloth tied to an arm.

American medics never carried guns. German medics normally didn't either. Sometimes though, German soldiers had placed the Red Cross bands on their sleeves to get closer to American soldiers, thereby setting them up for ambush. Germans also sometimes boobytrapped the dead bodies of their own soldiers. If Americans tried to move the corpse, they would be blown up.

Obviously, these had been German soldiers disguised as medics, hence the gun holsters. And whoever had originally found the bodies had tied strips of cloth to their arms to drag them a short distance to see if they had been boobytrapped.

Welcome to Germany, I thought.

We had a good airstrip at Sarreguemines — firm and long enough to land on without any problems. We pilots slept in tents erected alongside the runway. The weather remained good. We had no problem flying every day.

But the corpses lying just outside my tent bothered me at night. I had seen dead bodies before, and I had seen men killed. At Luneville, between our airstrip and the edge of the city was a sign on a stick indicating a grave of a German. Just beyond the P-47 landing strip was a burned-out tank with a German soldier's body hanging out of the turret. At Haguenau, there had been several bodies near the end of a landing strip. And so on. Battlefield death is tragic, but I did not dwell on it at the time — until now.

At night I lay awake on my cot. I could not get the dead bodies, just a few feet away, out of my mind. One night I had a panic attack. I broke out in a sweat and wanted to get up and run some where. But there was no place to run, and I knew there would be corpses wherever I went. I could not move. I believe that was the first time I really understood the true meaning of the position I was in. There was good reason for me to believe I would end up like those two German soldiers, whose bodies were rotting just a few feet from where I was sleeping.

I picked up a feeling of dread that stayed with me until the war was over. And at that point I wondered if the war would ever end.

On March 26, 1945, the 72nd Liaison Squadron moved on to Kaiserslautern, well into Germany. The whole situation changed. We were among the enemy.

We were told to find a house near the landing strip, run the family out, and move in. Several of us pilots found a very good house nearby. The door was locked, but we broke the latch and entered. The family was long gone, but they had left everything in its place.

First, we explored the house throughout. We knew the owners would be afraid to return until we had moved on. The dining room was well furnished, with a large dining table, a sideboard, and an elaborately decorated cupboard that was locked. Using my bayonet, which I carried in my duffle bag and had absolutely no use for, I chopped open the drawers and doors. A large set of fine silverware and glassware was inside. I had no use for either, but there was a box that held a silver carving set — just what I was looking for to hold my diaries. I dumped out the contents and took the box, in which I still store my diaries.

The house was full of Nazi literature, military paraphernalia, Nazi newspapers, military journals, and magazines.

We began to see the disintegration of the German army. Some members of our squadron said they had seen some unarmed German soldiers walking down a road. They were tired of fighting and were heading for home. One of our boys had been on guard duty when two German soldiers gave themselves up to him in the middle of the night. It was a lucky break for him; he took some good souvenirs from the Germans, namely their pistols. We also heard that a headquarters outfit was setting up at the time a group of Germans surrendered. Our soldiers were too busy to handle them, so they sent the Germans to the rear without escort.

At Kaiserslautern, a small private German aircraft was sitting just off our landing strip. I was the first pilot to look it over and in a compartment behind the pilot's headrest I found a Nazi flag in perfect shape, which I took.

Late one afternoon there, several of us pilots were standing on our landing strip when one of them pointed to the north.

"I've been watching that Cub over there for some time and all he seems to be doing is circling. Reckon something is going on over there?"

We all looked where he was pointing. About two miles away a Piper Cub was flying in circles. After a while, he turned away from us and flew

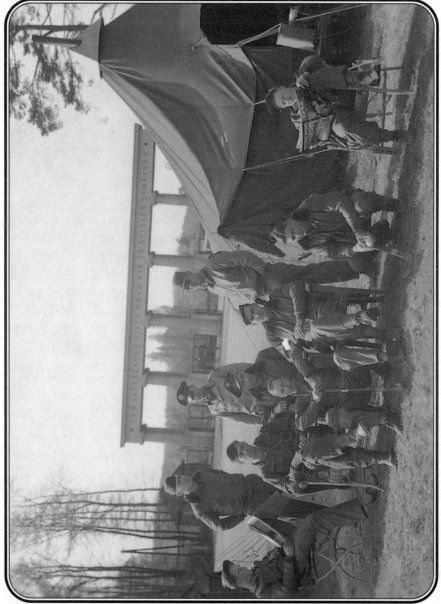

Pilots of the 72nd Liaison Squadron sitting in front of the Operations tent at Darmstadt, Germany. A German civilian was shot near the group by their guard. Technical Sergeant James R. Bryce is sitting third from the right.

into the distance. Turning west, he flew almost out of sight, then returned and circled a few more times. Finally, he turned toward us and flew to our strip and landed. He taxied to where we were and climbed out of his aircraft.

He was a First Lieutenant in the Artillery. We asked him why he was flying circles within sight of our strip.

"I was lost," he explained. We all thought that maybe he should have stuck to shooting cannon.

On April 2, 1945, the 72nd Liaison Squadron moved to Darmstadt. Our landing strip was on a field where German athletes had held field and track events. It was relatively small, but it served our purposes adequately. We took over several houses near the stadium complex and lived in comfort.

The German civilians were scared to death of American soldiers. When we walked in and took over their house, the people ran away like scared rats. They left without taking anything with them. When we dealt with a civilian, it was like dealing with a slave.

When we first had arrived in Darmstadt, a Lieutenant and I went into a bar for a beer. The barmaid, a middle-aged woman rather neat in appearance, approached us as if we were rattlesnakes. We had been warned that we might be served poison beer — a ridiculous warning. She knew immediately what we wanted. When she drew two mugs of beer, she made elaborate signs that the beer was safe — she even drank a gulp from each mug herself. I paid her with some money I had taken from a house in Kaiserslautern. She took it without looking. Later, I found it to be worthless. She had not said a word.

One of our pilots found a German officer's uniform, complete from boots to cap, including a dress sword. I tried it on, and it fit quite well. With those tall black boots, shiny sword, high-peaked cap, and a fresh haircut (I had just gotten my first one in weeks) I looked as Prussian as one of the members of the elite military Junkers family.

Our landing field at Darmstadt, on the edge of town, was no more than a grassy lot of about five acres. Before we had arrived, German civilians

Technical Sergeant James R. Bryce (r) stands in a chow line in Darmstadt, Germany.

had walked along a path across the field worn deep in the grass. After we set up Operations, we had placed guards all about, and the civilians were no longer allowed to cross the field.

One afternoon of a beautiful spring-like day, a group of us were sitting in front of our Operations tent talking about nothing in particular when we saw a civilian start across the field. He was only about 50 yards away and crossing at right angles to us. He was well dressed, wore a gray rain coat and snap-brim hat, and was carrying brown gloves in his left hand. He walked as though he was unaware the field was under guard.

Our guard started toward him from the other side of the field, walked about ten yards, and yelled, "Halt!" The man evidently did not hear him. The guard walked a few feet farther and yelled "Halt!" again. This time the fellow must have heard, for he looked up, but he did not stop walking.

The guard swung his rifle to his shoulder and began to back away from the approaching civilian. The civilian saw the gun leveled at him and reached inside his coat pocket. The guard fired and missed, then fired again before the man could breathe. The man fell flat on his face and rolled over onto his back. He began thrashing about as the guard, still holding the gun walked over to him. The civilian almost touched the guard's leg. The guard drew his gun back as though to strike a crushing blow. However, he did not strike the thrashing German. Instead he stepped back, cradled his gun in his arm, and stood quietly watching the dying German kick about on the ground.

All this happened about 50 yards from where we were sitting. A few birds were singing. We all jumped to our feet.

"I'll be damned! He shot him!" someone exclaimed.

Another soldier had come up behind us and had not seen the shooting. "Shot who?" he asked.

"That German civilian," someone else answered.

"Where?"

"Right out there on the ground, in front of that guard."

"Yeh, I see him. I'll be damned. I'll be damned."

One of our officers started walking toward the civilian. Someone else started a jeep standing beside the tent and drove toward the civilian. Several of us jumped on the passing jeep and rode to the guard. We arrived there at the same time as the officer.

The officer did not know what to do. He just stood and watched the wounded man kick. The German was very pale and pasty-looking from shock, and his eyes were damp from pain. He was not making much noise, just a grunt of pain occasionally. He would throw his arms wildly, then lie quietly for a while.

"I told him to halt, but he didn't, and he reached in his coat," the guard said quietly, not changing expression.

"Maybe he had a gun," the officer said. As if glad to find something to do, he unbuckled the German's raincoat and reached inside his jacket. There was no gun. The officer pulled out a leather folder full of ration stamps and an ID card.

By then, the Sergeant of the Guard had arrived.

"What are your orders in cases like this?" the officer asked the Sergeant of the Guard.

He didn't know. "He's a German civilian. Hell, he should have stopped," replied the Sergeant of the Guard.

"I don't know where to take him," the officer said.

I yelled for the ambulance sitting across the field.

"Yeh, get the ambulance," the officer said, as if he had just thought of it.

The medic drove the ambulance over. He climbed out and came over to the German.

"I don't know where to take him," he said. "I can't take a German civilian to a military hospital."

"Well, put him in the ambulance. We'll find some place to take him," answered the officer. "How about a civilian hospital?"

"They've all been bombed out," the medic replied.

"Well put him in the ambulance. We can't leave him out here," the officer said, and began walking back toward the tent.

We put the German on the stretcher and loaded him into the ambulance. The medic drove back across the field and parked beside the Operations tent. A crowd gathered at the back of the ambulance to see the wounded German. He was still waving his arms convulsively. His brown gloves were still grasped tightly in his left hand.

One of the officers called the Provost Marshal, told him what had happened, and asked for instructions.

"You don't want me," the Provost Marshal answered. "You want Graves Registration."

"But he isn't dead yet," our officer said.

"Oh, hell!" the Provost Marshal exclaimed, and was silent for a moment. Then he said, "Take him to the POW hospital." And that was that.

Our medical officer and the ambulance driver took the man to the POW cage and turned him in to the German POW medics. We learned later that he had died within two hours. The shot had punctured the lower part of his lung and he died of internal hemorrhage.

Back at the landing strip, the afternoon wore on. The guard was given the rest of the day off. We discussed the incident for a while, then began talking about girls. I flew one more mission before dark.

On April 10, 1945, I took an observer on a reconnaissance mission south of Darmstadt. I followed the Autobahn south to Heidelberg, then turned off to fly above the Neckar River through the hills toward Heilbronn. The observer wanted to find the front lines, to see if there was any action. I was paying attention to my flying, but not as much as I should have been, perhaps. Besides, everything looked pretty quiet.

I was flying at about 200 feet, when suddenly my L-5 rose about 100 feet with a loud explosion that had roared up from the ground. I looked down to see that I was directly over an American artillery battery. The concussion of the salvo they had just fired had tossed my aircraft up like a leaf. Ahead of me I saw the shells hit the German position. For the moment I was directly over No Man's Land, with nothing beneath me for protection except a few feet of clear air and the thin piece of my painted canvas fuselage.

Since we found the action we were looking for, I dove for the ground and hedgehopped out of there!

On April 12, 1945, I flew a mission to Neustadt, returning rather late in the afternoon. When I landed, a pilot met me as I pulled up to the flight line. He had a shocked look on his face.

"Roosevelt is dead," he said, rather quietly.

I couldn't believe it. I didn't want to believe it. It could not happen! Franklin D. Roosevelt had been my president as long as I could remember. When I was a child he had become a part of my consciousness. He had guided my country through the Great Depression and in preparation for war. His mighty voice had reassured a frightened population that everything would be all right. When the Japanese had bombed Pearl Harbor on December 7, 1941, President Roosevelt appeared before Congress the next day. With ringing oratory, he had declared our nation at war, and we knew we would win it! He had led our country throughout a long and hard conflict. It was not right that he would not preside over the greatest victory of arms any country in history had ever achieved. Victory was in sight, and President Roosevelt had guided us all the way, with firmness and care. I thought he surely could not be dead right now; but he was. The sense of loss was almost overpowering.

Chapter 14

O N APRIL 15, 1945, the 72nd Liaison Squadron moved to Kitzingen, and took over a major German airfield. The Operations building had been badly bombed. We were able to move into one of the hangar buildings and set up relatively acceptable living conditions.

The war in Europe was nearing its end. As martial control by the Nazis broke down in Germany and their occupied territories, there was basically no government. Allied bombing had taken its toll on industrial complexes and cities. Food and basic services were a scarcity for civilian as well as the military sectors.

As Germany had geared up for war, most able-bodied men had been drafted into the military. To replace the draftees in the work force, foreigners — "slave laborers" — had been brought in to do the hard labor, working in mines or building roads. Certain skilled laborers worked in the factories.

We were becoming aware of a unique situation unfolding in Germany. The roads were clogged with "displaced persons" from other countries, victims of the war. No relief agencies were functioning to help them, nor did they have any form of transportation, except to walk. They just wanted to get away from Germany and go home.

Many people on the road were Russian soldiers, who had been captured on the Eastern Front. When the Americans overran the Russian POW camps, the prisoners simply walked away. The Germans had made the Russian POWs wear degrading, striped prison garb, as if they were criminals. Thus, after they were liberated, the Russian soldiers frequently went cross-country looking for German farmers. When they found a farmer's house, in retaliation they usually looted, killed the family, and in many cases raped the women.

About 100 yards from where we were billeted, a group of about 200 displaced persons, mostly Russians, a few Poles, and Czechs were living in an abandoned German barrack. They were all a miserable lot, for they had very little to eat and had had no sanitary facilities since being freed from their German masters. I visited the place a couple of times. The barrack had no lights, and their toilet was the hallway. They cooked what food they could get on fires built outside the barrack.

There were plenty of girls in their early 20s at this barrack, so naturally soldiers visited every night. They danced in a small room. A violin player and an accordion player would begin their entertainment before sundown, and the people would begin crowding in to dance. A few soldiers would push into the smelly room, grab a likely looking girl, and try to dance to the strange music. As night came on, the room became darker and darker. Sweating, milling people danced more and more awkwardly and drunkenly, for much wine and champagne had been stolen from German warehouses.

Finally, the room would become almost dark, with only the glow of cigarettes. Then, the place suddenly took on the atmosphere of a pest hole. Strange voices mumbled and yelled out. The weird music sounded unholy. Soldiers would bump into hungry Russians and Poles. All would be holding or grabbing a girl who did not mind the most intimate contact.

All these people had been the victims of German cruelty for many years. Now that they were free, their happiness was unbounded and they expressed it with wild, uninhibited joy.

At this time I also saw truck convoys of American soldiers being transported to the front, as German soldiers were beginning to surrender. When these convoys returned, the trucks were loaded with young German POWs in new uniforms.

On April 27, 1945, we left Kitzingen and went to a place called Swabischgmund. On most maps it is usually abbreviated as Gmund. We stayed at Gmund only a couple of days. By the time we reached the town, it was even more obvious that Germany was going to lose the war.

On the same day, an event occurred that would forever mark Germany with the stain of pure evil. The soldiers of the Seventh Army, under General Alexander M. Patch, opened the death camp at Dachau, a small town a few miles north of Munich.

I had made a flight from Gmund to Darmstadt, arriving back late in the afternoon. As I pulled my L-5 up to the flight line, a pilot was just getting out of his aircraft. He bent over as he stepped to the ground and vomited. I thought he might be sick, and I went to see if I could help him.

"Are you sick?" I asked.

"They're piled on flat cars like cord wood."

"What?"

"Dead bodies," he said. "They piled dead bodies onto flat cars. They were trying to haul them off, I guess."

"What in the world are you talking about?"

"I took an officer to Dachau. It's a concentration camp and the Germans have killed thousands of people and there are dead bodies lying around all over the place. Dead bodies scattered everywhere. They're all naked and look like skeletons."

We all were told we could take the time to fly to Dachau. It was strictly a voluntary trip, but General Eisenhower had suggested that every American soldier who could, should go see these death camps. He wanted history to record the broad, deep depths of the evil to which the human race was capable of descending.

I did not avail myself of the opportunity. I had seen the horror on the face of my fellow pilot.

On May 2, 1945, we moved to Augsburg. When we arrived, the war was coming to an end. The German army in Italy had surrendered, Berlin was surrounded by Russian forces, and Hitler had committed suicide in his bunker in Berlin. More concentration camps had been found by the Allies. The full horror of what the Nazi regime had done was being revealed to the shocked world. The countryside and the roads were teeming with civilians, former slave laborers, and displaced persons, all trying to escape from where the Nazis had held them prisoners or from the constant bombardment of the American Armed Forces.

The fabric of German society was disintegrating. Victims of Nazi barbarity were telling their stories of the atrocities. To be a German at this time was to be hated by everyone. The opening of the death camps really did them in. That, and the fact that when the German army had marched victoriously across the face of Europe, they had pillaged, killed, tortured, and destroyed everything and everyone in their path.

The rule of law no longer applied to Germans. There was no protection for them. As the war ended, and the Allies moved across their land, the occupying military forces would not help them in any way as a matter of principle. After starting two world wars, ransacking nations, murdering civilians by the millions, and setting up death camps to destroy entire races of people, the Germans had forfeited their right to a position of decency and respect.

One small incident that I remember so well illustrates to me the German situation at the end of the war. No one really was physically hurt, but I remember it vividly.

On first arriving in Augsburg I was standing across the street from about five Russians, in prison-striped clothing, who must have just been released from a POW stockade. As a German teen-age girl rode past them on her bicycle, one of the Russians stepped off the curb. He knocked her off and onto to the street. He picked up the bicycle and straddled it. The girl shook her head to gather her wits about her. When she saw the Russian sitting on her bicycle, a look of fright and resignation came over her face, large tears filled her eyes. She did not say a word. She just walked away whimpering. Many people were on the street and, like myself, had seen what happened; but no one cared. The Russians wandered off down the street with the thief riding slowly along with his newly acquired bicycle. There was not one thing the girl could do about it, and no one would help her.

While in Augsburg, flying became very interesting. We were taking off from a good airfield next to a bombed-out Messerschmitt plant. Spring was arriving, and almost every day the weather was beautiful for flying. Most of our missions were to the southeast toward Munich and beyond. Bavaria was a rolling countryside of low hills that grew higher until they blended into the Alps visible in the distance.

And most of the missions were very interesting. For instance, I carried a Major to Lechfield, due south of Augsburg on May 4, 1945. He was to examine Messerschmitt Me-262 jets and Me-163 Komet rocket-powered fighters based there. The Me-262 was the first operational turbojet-powered fighter aircraft in history — Hitler's "secret weapon." It had gone into service in mid-1944. If it had come along earlier and been used to its greatest advantage, the air war could have changed drastically. The speed of the Me-262 was phenomenal. The American P-51s escorting our bomber squadrons could not catch the Me-262s. When the jet attacked a formation of B-17s, they dove in, blasted, and flew away before the P-51 pilots could respond. However, neither the Me-262 nor the Me-163 were manufactured in significant numbers before the end of the war in 1945.

The Me-163, I believe, was the only rocket-powered aircraft ever flown in combat, but it still was in the developmental stage. Because of its limited fuel capacity, it had a unique attack mode. When a flight of bombers appeared, the Me-163 would take off and climb above the bombers on its initial power thrust. Then, with its fuel almost exhausted, the pilot would cut power and dive down on the formation of bombers. He could only make one run at them. Still, the escort of P-51s could not protect against the Me-163.

Shortly after our arrival at Augsburg, the highest-ranking Nazi left alive, the man who was Hitler's right-hand man, and the man Hitler had chosen to succeed him, was captured south of Augsburg — Field Marshal Hermann Wilhelm Goering. Goering had been a flying ace in World War I. When Baron Manfred von Richtofen — the "Red Baron" — had been killed, Goering became commander of Richtofen's Flying Circus, the most famous group of German fighter pilots during that war.

Goering had joined the Nazi party in 1922. When Hitler had come to power, Goering built the *Luftwaffe* into one of the most powerful air forces in history, until the United States entered the war.

I really wanted to take a look at this person. Field Marshal Goering was no small potatoes, I tell you. I arrived where he was being held early in the morning. He was standing on the tarmac near our Operations section. A small group of soldiers, standing a short distance away from him, was there for the same reason I was. They wanted to see the man.

Goering was being held at the airfield awaiting an aircraft to carry him to Luxembourg where he was to be initially incarcerated.

Goering was a big man, but his soft-blue uniform was so well tailored he did not look obese. He wore tan boots. He stood with his feet rather wide apart, and seemed in a jolly mood.

I found odd the behavior of a little man carrying an opera cape, hovering about Goering like a moth. He would occasionally step up and slip the cape over Goering's shoulders, then step back for a moment, then step forward and remove the cape. After a minute or two he would repeat the performance.

Then, I witnessed a sight I could not believe. As U.S. officers approached the prisoner, they snapped a smart salute. Goering always returned the salute, then would stick out his hand. The American officers would shake hands with him. Goering was a murderous Nazi who deserved no respect from anyone, certainly not American soldiers.

When word got out that American officers were showing such courtesies to Field Marshal Goering, General Alexander Patch put a stop to such practices immediately.

It was reported that when General Patch confronted Goering upon his capture, Patch took Goering's Marshal baton from his grasp. Goering was offended.

"I must keep my baton," Goering is reported to have said. "It is the symbol of my authority."

"You have no authority," Patch is reported to have replied.

Finally an aircraft taxied up and Goering was led aboard for the flight to Luxembourg. During the Nuremberg War Trials in November of 1945, he was found guilty of crimes against humanity and sentenced to be hanged. However he cheated the hangman's noose by committing suicide in 1946.

On May 8, 1945, I flew a mission carrying an officer to Wiesbaden. While he went into town, I stayed in my L-5 listening to the radio, and heard that President Harry S. Truman was going to speak. I was very lucky. I heard the entire speech quite clearly. Truman was broadcasting live to the entire world. He announced that the war in Europe was at an end, and that Germany had surrendered unconditionally.

I had no idea how to react. I just sat there and listened. We had all known for days that the European war was almost over. There was hardly anything left in Germany to bomb. But there had been many times when I had thought the war might never end, and now with the finality, I felt numb.

When President Truman had finished his speech, orders followed that were to be broadcast continually for the next two days.

"All military personnel, cease fire and hold your position. All military personnel, cease fire and hold your position."

That message was repeated for hours over and over on American Armed Forces radio, with breaks in between filled by Big Band music.

When my passenger returned, as he crawled into my aircraft, he remarked, "I guess you heard the news." I acknowledged that I had.

I took off and headed back to Augsburg. I was barely out of sight of Wiesbaden when I became aware that I was not alone in the skies. I had climbed to about 2,000 feet. As I flew along I began to notice B-17s and B-24s all over the sky, at many different altitudes. They were not in any formation; they were just wandering about over Germany. Other pilots flying that day also noticed the same phenomenon.

I soon learned that the bomber commands in England and Italy had allowed the crews to load up their aircraft with ground personnel who had been servicing the bombers all during the war. They wanted to see what the bombing had done to Germany. On the day the war ended, they were given a good look. I'll bet they were impressed.

With the war over, flying became much more interesting in the ideal spring weather. Bavaria was beautiful. The Alps, their peaks still snow-covered, formed a background for a countryside that looked like a calendar landscape.

Hitler's chalet, named Berghof, was near the alpine village of Berchtesgaden, a few miles south of Salzburg, Austria. Situated high in the mountains with a beautiful view, it immediately became a tourist attraction.

On May 12, 1945, I carried a Lieutenant General Ortiz of the Mexican army to Salzburg. He and other "tourists" were transported by military vehicle to Berchtesgaden and farther up the mountain to visit Hitler's chalet.

I knew General Ortiz would not return for several hours, and thus I had the time to fly to Berchtesgaden and gaze down upon the home of Adolf Hitler. However, I had seen so much already that I decided a nap would be more refreshing. While I waited the return of the Mexican General, I stretched out under the wing of my L-5 and slept. I missed my only chance to see Hitler's chalet, but I do not feel deprived.

My flights to Innsbruck, Austria, were dramatic and inspiring. Only from a plane could one really capture the real beauty of that countryside in the spring. On leaving Augsburg, I first passed near several clear, blue lakes, then, as I flew farther south, the Alps came into view in the distance. As I approached the mountains, however, I realized I could not fly over them in my L-5.

At Garmisch-Partenkirchen I found a road and railroad to follow, through lowest valleys. I flew about 1,000 feet above the ground. On each side of the railroad the mountains rose thousands of feet. The up-drafts and down-drafts tossed my little L-5 around like a leaf. But I never felt in danger, because I kept my distance from the mountains and held enough altitude to take the down-drafts in stride.

As I flew farther, I passed over several villages, so far removed from the war that there was no damage of any kind. They had looked the same as they had in peacetime, for hundreds of years.

Suddenly in front of me was a deep, wide valley. I could not see the bottom of it at first, but then I passed over a little village named Seefeld. The railroad I had been following disappeared into a tunnel to my left. I came out over the valley of the Inn River, at about 2,500 feet. I dove down toward Innsbruck off to my left. I glanced at the sheer cliffs of the mountains through which I had just passed. Up on the sheer cliffs were the railroad tracks I had been following. A train on these tracks was just entering a tunnel cut into the sheer cliff. I was flying lower than the train.

I landed on a dirt strip on the east side of Innsbruck, after a wonderful trip.

A glassy-blue lake, Zell am See, a few miles south of Salzburg, sits at the junction of two green Alpine valleys and reflects the ever-changing shadows of the eternal Alps. Its smooth surface is never agitated beyond a few ripples made by toy-like sailboats that move very slowly about its surface, propelled by the light breezes sweeping down from the mountain peaks. The crest of a mountain seems to bend its majestic back and run downward into the lake. There it touches the water and disappears beneath the cool surface.

The town of Zell an See seems more like soft moss on a great log that has fallen into a mirror stream than a village made by mortal man. So beautiful, so remote, and so lacking in the ragged associations a person gathers in a war, the town was the end of the road for the American Seventh Army in its long campaign that had started on the beaches of the Riviera in southern France.

I landed at a small airfield just south of town. I taxied back to the edge of the field and cut my engine. I was not prepared for what I saw. Immediately, several dozen German soldiers gathered about and began staring at me and my L-5. They were a dirty-looking lot; their uniforms were in varying degrees of raggedness and filth. All of them needed a shave.

I crawled out and motioned them to back away. They obeyed, without saying a word. I could tell they were accustomed to taking orders. Across the field were several dozen German vehicles of all shapes and models, lined up in more or less an orderly manner. I could see smoke coming from a few of the chimneys sticking out the roofs of several house trailers. Then I saw some women in the trailers. The sight of those women with their defeated men struck me as incongruous. In the remnants of a beaten army, a woman looks as out of place as anything I can think of.

A German officer came over to my L-5. His uniform was in good repair, but very dirty and wrinkled. His coat was buttoned and all his medals pinned on. His face was pale and thin. He stood there for a long time and stared at me and my aircraft, but I do not think he saw me. He had a blank expression on his face.

I had flown to Zell am See to pick up an American Colonel and take him back to Augsburg. When he arrived, he noticed I was studying the Germans. He joined me and was silent for a short while.

Then the Colonel said, "What a motley bunch of vehicles. No standardization, absolutely no standardization whatsoever."

His comment struck me as being a peculiar remark to make about the very regimented German army.

I took off, and we flew north up the valley and away from the field that had become a mausoleum for the remnants of our enemy. As the sordid sight faded in the distance, we seemed to gather the beauty of the snow-capped peaks about us and draw relief from the view of the green valleys that passed below us.

Afterword

ON JUNE 4, 1945, we left Augsburg and returned to Darmstadt. I did not realize it at the time, but I had gone as far as I would in this war. We had been in Darmstadt two weeks and had not flown our L-5s. We were told that the next day we were to turn our aircraft in at an Army depot. It was difficult for me to realize that I would not have a plane to fly anymore.

On June 20, 1945, I got into my L-5 for the last time, pulled on my parachute harness, strapped my seat belt in place, and took off with nine other pilots of the 72nd Liaison Squadron. We were headed for Creil, France, about 30 miles north of Paris. The flight was interesting. We crossed four different countries. We took off from Darmstadt, Germany, flew across the small country of Luxembourg, just north of the city of Luxembourg, then crossed the extreme southern border of Belgium before finally entering France.

As we approached the landing field at Creil, I witnessed

another phenomenon only associated with World War II. Stretched out in rows on both sides of the landing strip were hundreds of military aircraft — P-47s, B-25s, B26s, Piper Cubs, and L-5s. We circled the field and landed. A man on the ground directed us to tie-down places. I pulled into the indicated slot, cut my engine, and sat silently in my aircraft for a moment. Then I unbuckled my seat belt, slipped out of my parachute harness, and climbed out.

I was losing my L-5. I had spent many hours in that aircraft, and we had shared some pretty good adventures. I stood beside it for a moment; I kissed my fingertips and touched the cowling. Then I walked away.

It was the last time I ever piloted an aircraft.

The road home was long, but we were glad to take it. We left Darmstadt in a truck convoy for a staging area called Camp New York. From there, we went by train to Brest, France, where we boarded a ship for Camp Shanks, New York. I took a train for San Antonio, Texas, then rode a bus on to my home and my parents in Wichita Falls. The trip home had been a small saga in its own right.

I was given a 30-day "convalescent" furlough. While I was home, atomic bombs were dropped on Hiroshima on August 6th, then on Nagasaki three days later, ending the war in the Pacific. Japan surrendered on August 15, 1945. World War II had finally come to its conclusion.

Immediately, the U.S. Army began the process of discharging the troops on the basis of a point system, determined by length of service and the number of medals and citations.

I had received a Presidential citation that had been given to the entire 72nd Liaison Squadron. In addition, I had a European Campaign ribbon with Palms for the Rome-Arno campaign; the invasion of southern France campaign; the Rhineland campaign; and the Germany campaign. I also had the Air Medal with Three Palms, and the Good Conduct Medal. And two "hash marks" on my left sleeve denoted my length of service, all of which gave me plenty of points for a discharge.

The war was over, I had the points, so I took the discharge.

$\mathcal{I}ndex$

by Lori L. Daniel